# KITCHEN TABLE GIVING: REIMAGINING HOW CONGREGATIONS CONNECT WITH THEIR DONORS

## WILLIAM G. ENRIGHT

"*Kitchen Table Giving* reflects the new paradigm of charitable giving. With grace-bearing words, Bill Enright transports the reader to a generative place to discover the joy of preaching and teaching about giving. He exquisitely weaves through this book insightful stories, cutting-edge research, thoughtful questions and wonderful principles. The joy of giving, in a vision-inspired and value-driven fashion, frames Enright's insightful engagement. *Reimagining How Congregations Connect With Their Donors* is aspirational as well as informative, inspirational and invitational."

**David Daniels III, Henry Winters Luce Professor of World Christianity, McCormick Seminary. Bishop, Church of God in Christ.**

"*Kitchen Table Giving* is much more than another how-to book about fundraising. It is a blueprint for entering the sacred spaces where God's leading, a congregation's vision and the heart of a donor interconnect and bear fruit. This is an important and inspiring work for two reasons. First, it empowers congregations to embrace fundraising as a form of ministry, rather than a chore. Second, this easy-to-read book introduces faith communities to an approach to fundraising that works!"

**Henry Freeman, President, H. Freeman Associates, LLC**

"Drawing on decades of experience, Bill Enright understands as deeply as anyone that religious fundraising is about ministry and discipleship more than money. This timely and important book will catalyze rich giving conversations."

**Richard Gunderman, Chancellor's Professor, Philanthropy and Medical Humanities, Indiana University**

# WHAT CLERGY SAY ABOUT KITCHEN TABLE GIVING

"In *Kitchen Table Giving*, Bill Enright has provided a rich feast to fuel both personal transformation and growth in transformational leadership around financial stewardship and fundraising for the sake of God's mission in the world. Culled from many years of adept leadership, Bill's deep theological insight and skilled biblical interpretation blend engagingly with compelling stories and sound research. At the end of each chapter probing questions draw readers into deep conversations that will inspire and make a lasting difference in the lives of individuals and congregations. I'll be sharing this fine book with as many congregational leaders as I can.

**William O. Gafkjen, Bishop, Indiana-Kentucky Synod, ELCA.**
**Chair, ELCA Conference of Bishops**

"*Kitchen Table Giving* offers a wise, deep and joyful approach to cultivating a culture of generosity as Bill Enright shows us the way to uncover dreams and give voice to the silent longings of our hearts. This exceptional and timely book is a must-read for every pastor and non-profit leader who is called to steward the potential God has given them."

**Bishop Janice Riggle Huie, (Retired) United Methodist Church**
**Texas Methodist Foundation, Leadership Formation**

"A master storyteller, Bill Enright writes as a pastor and fundraising teacher so that leaders of congregations and Christian organizations know what to do and why it is important. He lets readers know what it takes to be a trustworthy spiritual leader who talks about giving as part of the life of faith. This book inspires and gives practical tips."

**David L. Odom, Executive Director: Leadership Education at Duke Divinity**

"Ministry needs money. It is God's gift that helps a congregation accomplish good things. Yet, many of us find money-talk challenging. Bill Enright's excellent book enables clergy and laity to experience fundraising as relational wisdom. Sit down and read this book with others and you will be better prepared to talk about one of the most important matters of faith: generosity."

**Tim Shapiro, President, Indianapolis Center for Congregations.**

"Stewardship is changing for the church today but Bill Enright reminds us that it is still about mission and relationships. This book helps congregations see that the locus of giving conversations is the donor's table; the challenge for leadership is getting a seat at the table. The exercises at the end of each chapter are wonderful guides for helping pastors and stewardship leaders make the paradigm shifts necessary to grow generosity in the church. It will be on the agenda at our next Generosity Team meeting."

**Tom Walker, Senior Pastor, Palms Presbyterian Church,**
**Jacksonville Beach, FL. Board Chair, Columbia Theological Seminary**

"Here is a 21st century handbook of hope designed to move us from the front porch of 'asking' to the kitchen table where soul-talk births generous giving. Bill Enright artfully takes us beyond money to ministry as he addresses one of the most challenging issues facing the church today: Giving."

**T. Garrott Benjamin, Senior Pastor Emeritus, Light of the World Christian Church. Distinguished Adjunct Professor, Wesley Seminary, Indiana Wesleyan University**

"God's mission all too often goes severely underfunded because pastors and boards have not learned the essentials of getting to the "ask." Dr. Enright's broad experience blended with his rich wisdom and insight offer the corrective. *Kitchen Table Giving* belongs in every pastor's and stewardship/fundraising team's toolkit."

**Lynn Cheyney, Senior Pastor, Westwood Presbyterian Church, Los Angeles, CA**

"Bill Enright has been a keen observer of the changing patterns, motivations and dynamics of religious giving. *Kitchen Table Giving* is a must read for clergy and laity who want to transform the way congregations and religious organizations think about money and religious fundraising."

**Lewis F. Galloway, Senior Pastor, Second Presbyterian Church, Indianapolis, IN**

"Bill Enright has invited us to the kitchen table for conversation, learning, and giving. He uses decades of learning and teaching about generosity and stewardship to help the reader examine opportunities and challenges for giving in a time of rapid change and transition. Joining together spiritual inquiry, sound research, and poignant narratives, Dr. Enright opens a way for learning and transformation. This table book is a gift to all us… leaders, clergy, inquiring followers, children of God. Truly, the kitchen table described in this writing is God's table where we are nourished by God's abundance and love and sustained for generous response and hopeful life."

**James B. Lemler, Rector (retired) of Christ Church Greenwich, CT. Vice President of the Allen Whitehall Clowes Charitable Foundation**

"Generosity in financial giving is the engine that drives the mission and ministry of congregations. Bill Enright hits all the right notes in *Kitchen Table Giving*. The stories alone are worth the book, and the hope they stimulate of vibrant and generous congregations gives me renewed enthusiasm for the future of the church."

**George A Mason, Senior Pastor, Wilshire Baptist Church, Dallas, Texas**

# CONTENTS

# ACKNOWLEDGEMENTS

A book does not one person write; books are often mirrors of the author's life. *Kitchen Table Giving* reflects the lessons, learnings and insights of hundreds of people: family, friends, professional colleagues, mentors and students. I am grateful for the people whose imprint sits large in this book.

- I am thankful for the generosity of the late Karen Lake Buttrey and her husband, Don, whose vision gave birth to the Lake Institute on Faith & Giving.
- I am thankful for my mentors and former colleagues at the Lake Institute on Faith & Giving and the Lilly Family School of Philanthropy at Indiana University, whose influence led to me to write this book: Founding Dean Gene Tempel; Tim Seiler, director emeritus of The Fundraising School; David King, Karen Lake Buttrey Director of the Lake Institute; Richard Klopp and Aimee Laramore my former associate directors.
- My special thanks to the staff of the Religion Division of Lilly Endowment, whose conversations over a quarter-century have been formative in the way I have come to think about faith, money and giving: Chris Coble, Craig Dykstra, Robert Lynn and John Wimmer.
- I am grateful for my professional peers who read the manuscript and made suggestions that have strengthened and clarified the final text: Henry Freeman, Emory Griffin, David King, Aimee Laramore, Tom Locke, Joan Malick, Lyn Milan, Tim Shapiro, Tom Walker and John Wimmer.
- Editors enable authors to read better than they write. My deep thanks to Holly Miller, who has done that for me.
- This book was a family project. My wife, Edie, read every draft with the eyes of a loving critic. Conversations with my son Scott and his wife Lisa broadened my understanding relative to church giving. Most of all, I am indebted to my writer-son Kirk, who walked beside me from beginning to end and whose wisdom shaped the layout of the book, and his wife Jeanette who finalized the design of the book cover.

I am a blessed man and I pray that this book will bless each reader and congregation.

# AUTHOR'S NOTE

The crow's nest from which I have viewed religious giving and fundraising for the past forty years has been that of a pastor and an academic practitioner. Following more than thirty years as a pastor, I was privileged to serve as the founding director of the Lake Institute on Faith & Giving, part of the Lilly Family School of Philanthropy at Indiana University. During those twelve years, my colleagues and I worked with more than 3,500 religious congregations and faith-based nonprofits. In addition, I monitored more than two hundred research projects for individuals pursuing a professional certificate in religious fundraising. What did I learn and observe from this life-altering perch?

In a sentence, religious fundraising is more about ministry than it is about money. Congregational-based fundraising is about relationships, trust, vision and growing informed disciples of Jesus Christ. As ministry, fundraising is essentially relational. It begins with listening: listening to how people talk about money, the language they use when talking about their church and its programs. When leaders in a congregation begin to listen, something revelatory happens. They find themselves looking at the congregation they serve through the eyes of their giving partners who are the congregation. Simply put, the focus of congregation-based fundraising is not so much on money as on sparking conversations that will birth a culture of thoughtful and generous disciples.

Congregations that ignore the ministry dimension of fundraising usually embark on a fundraising practice best described as "front porch giving." Once or twice a year they turn Jesus's words regarding prayer into a fundraising mantra: "Ask and it will be given to you, seek and you will find, knock and the door will be opened." (Matthew 7:7) So, for a Sunday or two, they ask and state their needs with the expectation that in asking they will receive. Yes, you should ask and pray, but fundraising is so much more than asking and praying. People no longer give just because the church asks. Effective religious fundraising hinges on what has been happening within the congregation before the "ask" is ever made. Generous giving turns on the kinds of conversations giving partners have had with themselves, their families and their friends. The front porch metaphor for fundraising is increasingly ineffective because it reflects a donor and a world that no longer exists. In the neighborhood where I live, the front porch has been scaled back to a mere entry way, often replaced by a back porch patio where privacy rules.

The next time you are in church, note the offering plate as it passes you by. What does it tell you about giving in your congregation? The traditional church envelope is increasingly passé as donors now utilize alternative payment methods such as automatic bank transfers, credit cards, mobile giving apps, etc. Giving decisions are made elsewhere. For many families, that place is back home at the kitchen table. For younger donors, it is the rarefied world of cyberspace with its on-the-spot allure that shapes their giving decisions. Therein sits the challenge of religious fundraising: How do we engage donors in conversation and share with them our story? How do we bridge the chasm between the pew and the giver's table, the church and the cloud of cyberspace? How might we better shape the conversations donors have with themselves when making a charitable decision?

I have written this book in the hope that it will serve as a practical guide for clergy and the stewardship leaders of congregations. Each chapter ends with a section titled "Table Talk" that includes issues for clergy, church leaders and stewardship committees to ponder, first individually, then together. "Table Talk" concludes with action steps to pursue as leaders apply the insights of each chapter to their congregational setting. The stories I share are true and reflect a variety of  research projects.  I only changed the names and locations of the stories to preserve the anonymity of the congregations involved.

*William G. Enright*

# (1)

## THE HIDDEN POWER OF TABLE TALK

*"As they sat at their table their eyes were opened and they recognized him."*
*Luke 24:30-31*

Late in my career as a pastor I woke up to the ways that conversations shape donors' giving habits. One cold December morning in 1996 my friend Tom called to ask if he might drop by for a chat that would take no more than fifteen minutes. True to his word Tom quickly cut to the issue: "Bill, you and I have been talking about the need in our church and denomination for young clergy. Well, Marjorie and I have also been talking; we think it's time to stop talking and begin doing." With that he handed me an envelope containing a large check with the charge to do something to address the issue and a request that the gift remain anonymous.

Fast forward two years. It's another cold December afternoon and Tom is again sitting in my office. With his and Marjorie's gift we had created a program in which each year two young clergy persons, fresh out of seminary, joined our staff for a two-year residency program focusing on parish ministry. Again Tom began, "Marjorie and I have been talking, and we want to keep the program going." He then handed me another envelope containing an even larger check.

That experience sparked my curiosity. Why did this always happen in December, and what

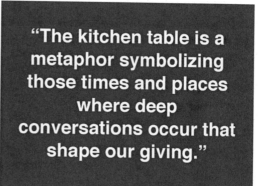

"The kitchen table is a metaphor symbolizing those times and places where deep conversations occur that shape our giving."

did Marjorie and Tom talk about as they made their giving decisions? Sometime later I discovered that every year around Thanksgiving Tom and Marjorie sat down at their kitchen table to sort through and finalize their charitable giving priorities: how much to give, to whom and why.

Where does effective religious fundraising begin? For many it begins with conversations around the kitchen table! The Gates Foundation began at the kitchen table of Bill Gates Sr. as he sat sorting through a variety of charitable requests before writing the foundation's first check, $80,000, to a local cancer program. Looking back on "Pledge Sunday" in the congregations I served, I recall that most people came to church with their pledge cards already filled out, bearing witness to earlier conversations. When I asked participants in our seminars where and how they made their charitable-giving decisions, those who were married replied: "At the kitchen table in conversation with my spouse." Research confirms the strategic role conversations play in traditional family life.

# 60%

**of donors make charitable-giving
decisions with spouse or partner[1]**

The Bible is replete with stories mirroring the importance of table talk in everyday life. The Old Testament tells the story of aging Abraham and childless Sarah laughing in mock disbelief as three visitors sitting at their kitchen table inform them of the impending birth of a child. In Luke's story of the resurrection, the gloom of Jesus's death is shattered when two heartbroken disciples invite a fellow traveler to sit at their table and then discover that the stranger is the Risen Christ.

In Christian literature, Martin Luther's classic *Table Talk* underscores the life-changing power of kitchen table conversations. In Luther's household, supper was served at five o'clock in the afternoon with visitors, students and university colleagues frequently joining Luther and his family for the meal. The conversation could be "jovial" as well as "animated" as Luther held court on issues ranging from religious beliefs and church politics to sex and marriage and clergy salaries and excessive interest rates. Looking back, one student wrote: "We used to call his conversation the condiments of the meal because we preferred it…to food."[2]   It was the conversation that made the table a life-shaping experience.

The kitchen table is a metaphor symbolizing those times and places where deep conversations occur that shape our charitable giving. My focus is not on the physicality of the table but on what occurs around the table. For example, I think of Starbucks with its table arrangement encouraging social conversations. I think of those serendipitous moments when we sit down with ourselves or a close friend and engage in soul-talk as we ponder what it means to live well and care generously. Giving conversations take many forms: public, private, formal, informal, human and even nonhuman, given the enigma of artificial intelligence.  The question church leaders need to ask themselves is this: How do we become a part of this tangle of giving conversations?

Today's giving table is as mobile as it is stationary.  When I asked one couple how they made their annual church pledge decision they replied, "Driving to and from Sunday church."  Think about that! It is in their cars coming and going that people reflect on their church experience, and those conversations ultimately influence their giving decisions.

Today's kitchen table frequently has a social, even clubby, persona about it. I'm thinking of social networks, what in congregational life we call "small groups." These are places of trust and accountability where people feel free to share their lives and stories. My wife and I volunteer in our congregation's food pantry.  One night we were having dinner with a group of friends when the subject of the food pantry came up.  Instantly, two people expressed strong views as to the validity of the ministry.  Some weeks later I noted that one of the silent listeners at the table had become a volunteer. The extended family is another frequently overlooked social network that plays a role in giving. When twenty and thirty year olds were asked what motivated them to give, 89 percent said their parents, 63 percent cited their grandparents.[3]

For many people, social media have become that invisible table where heart-wrenching messages arrest the soul and cause spur-of-the-moment acts of generosity. A tweet from a group of friends can raise money for a particular cause. My granddaughter texted me to support her participation in a dance marathon to raise money for a children's hospital. With a simple click, I can go to the GoFundMe website and support a cause that resonates with my passions—from accidents to illnesses to celebrations to graduations.

Today's giving table is more than a piece of furniture around which people gather. It's a human artifact composed of skin and bone and sacred memories. Its many forms and diverse character reflect a cultural reality that is reshaping the entire charitable giving landscape and dramatically altering church giving.

Since the late 20th century we have been experiencing what historian George McCully describes as a paradigm shift in charitable giving.[4]

1. Fundraising has been professionalized.
2. The number of nonprofits seeking funding has grown dramatically.
3. Charitable giving is now about opportunities, not obligations.
4. Technology has become a defining influence with the church envelope being upended by various forms of online giving.
5. The internet and website have replaced the telephone and snail mail as a primary means of communication.

Once upon a time, the priest or preacher could mount the pulpit, state a need and people would give. Today, donor giving is often more value-driven than need-driven with fundraising increasingly donor-centered rather than institution-centered.

Several years ago I was leading a day-long seminar for presidents of theological schools and seminaries in North America. After sharing with them this emerging paradigm, I asked what they saw to be the theological implications of this change. The group included Catholics and Protestants,

Evangelicals, Pentecostals and Mainline religious leaders and, truth be told, I looked forward to what I thought might be a controversial discussion. They called my bluff and in a matter of minutes unanimously gave their answer. They said, "In our fundraising we must learn to embody and mirror a theology of grace rather than a theology of duty and moral obligation!"

What does this paradigm shift portend for the local congregation? I see it affecting congregational giving in three ways.

First, as a result of this shift, the charitable giving pie is sliced into new portions. Traditionally, religious organizations such as congregations and denominations received the largest piece of the pie. Since 1990 the size of the piece of pie going to traditional religious communities has been reduced from one-half to one-third. For congregations, however, the news is not all doom and gloom.

# 74%

**of all religious organizations reported an
increase in giving in 2015[5]**

Giving to religion (congregations, denominations, missionary societies) continues to be the single largest recipient of charitable dollars. In 2016 religious giving increased 3 percent.[6] In the meantime, total charitable giving in the next few years is expected to grow by 3.6 percent in 2017 and 3.8 percent in 2018, exceeding the past ten year rate of growth.[7] The challenge for congregations is to learn how to make their case so they can claim more of their share of the giving pie.

Second, the explosion in the number of faith-based nonprofits has resulted in increased competition for the Almighty's Dollar. Religious donors now have more charitable giving choices than in any period of human history.

Between 1995 and 2010, the number of registered public charities increased 78 percent. The number of churches increased 92 percent. The number of para-church organizations—religious missions and ministries beyond the traditional church and denomination—increased 195 percent.[8] No longer may congregations and denominations assume that just because they ask, people will give. Donors are weighing the merits of many giving requests. Congregations must learn how to demonstrate their worthiness to receive the gifts they desire and deserve.

> **"Faith-motivated donors want to know: 'How in my giving can I support what God is about in the world?'"**

Third, the paradigm shift has expanded donors' giving horizons, birthing a new understanding to the nature of religious giving. Donors increasingly see religious giving as giving to any institution or mission that embodies their own spiritual or religious values. This includes gifts to secular organizations as well as religious nonprofits and congregations.

# 73%

**of all charitable dollars given by individuals go to organizations the donor perceives as having a religious or spiritual-related mission[9]**

Religious giving is global as well as local. Members of U.S. churches and synagogues send four and a half times as much money overseas every year as does the Gates Foundation.[10]

When viewed through the lens of this new paradigm, religious giving is not waning. It is flourishing, miming the wisdom of the psalmist: "The earth is the Lord's...the world and everything in it." (Psalm 34:1) For the local church, this means that congregational-based mission programs are pivotal to fundraising success.

Under the old paradigm, charitable giving may have been "sluggish in scope and spirit," but donors knew to whom they were giving and why.[11] Today religious giving is largely uninformed. Church givers feel overwhelmed by the causes seeking their support and are often ignorant as to how a mission or congregation uses its money. While more sophisticated givers may have a giving strategy and a charitable giving budget, most givers simply create their own rules of thumb as they go.[12] Needed by all is guidance. What does it mean to be a faithful steward? What does the Bible and a person's faith tradition have to say about God, money and giving?

For the past thirteen years I have been blessed with an insider's look at congregational life, how people give and why. There are:

- individuals who give joyfully based on friendship and their relationship with their pastor or involvement in a mission program or ministry of the church.
- a silent majority who automatically pledge the same amount they gave the previous year.
- people who give when there is a need, albeit, as one interviewee put it, "begrudgingly, just to do my fair share as a member."
- a growing number who attend but neither pledge nor give.
- couples who do their charitable giving separately so one year one partner may give to the church and one may not.
- a much smaller number who give generously with their generosity based on a discerned understanding of the tithe.

My mother was a tither—a single parent with a modest income and a heart for what God was about in the world. While it was her commitment to tithing that determined her giving, prayer was her discerning principle as to where to give. But prayer was more than a private conversation she had with herself and God; it was also a public conversation I overheard her have with her mother.

What sets congregations apart from most nonprofits is this: They have a spiritual access to table talk that is unique. Each week in worship they are blessed with a captive audience. When they embark on a fundraising program, they are engaging their members in a conversation that is as personal as it is public. Such public fundraising conversations should be informative, inspirational and invitational, with stories told that leave donors shouting a silent, "Wow, so that is what we are doing!" In contrast, many church fundraising programs fail because they are driven by a sense of urgency. Urgency does not make for good fundraising practices.

Years ago I was part of a consultation involving prominent religious leaders from a variety of Christian traditions. As the conference neared its end, a leader who had been rather silent throughout the conversation bared his soul. "In my religious tradition," he said, "fundraising is intentionally emotional and need-based. We tend to view fundraising as a necessary evil. To get money, we fan the flame of spiritual guilt and commitment. Our hope is that the flame will ignite a wildfire of impulsive giving with emotion serving as the midwife for generous giving. That approach is no longer working."

> "Many church fundraising programs fail because they are driven by a sense of urgency."

Religious institutions have a long history of harnessing their fundraising to the chariots of guilt or obligation. Romans Catholics have often associated fundraising with what they called the "begging sermon."[13] Protestant giving is frequently a mirror for what researchers call "comfortable guilt."[14] Duty does not inspire generous giving. In the face of guilt, people tend to give just enough to assuage their conscience. Ironically, many of those same people say that they are capable of giving more than they do![15]

Where then does thoughtful and generous giving begin? It begins by taking seriously the questions sitting center-stage in the minds of faith-driven donors. Faith-motivated donors want to know: "How in my giving can

I support what God is about in the world?" Smart congregational leaders address that question by telling stories that are more aspirational than preachy to spark the spiritual imaginations of their audience.

Savvy church leaders are people who listen to the longings of the hearts of those who have been entrusted to their care. It is in listening, in overhearing, that they become part of their donors' giving conversations. Congregations that seize this moment of opportunity set the table for the conversation donors will have with themselves at the giving tables of their lives.

Once religious leaders learn how to talk about faith, money, mission and giving in life-addressing conversations, something transformational happens within congregations.

- The taboo of money-talk in the church is obliterated.
- Fundraising becomes a spiritual ministry.
- Church leaders view their givers as mission partners rather than donors.
- Generosity becomes a practice of Christian discipleship.
- The fundraising focus is not on money but on the mission we share and the difference we can make together in God's world.
- People begin to talk with excitement as to what their church is about.
- Reclaimed is the biblical emphasis on money as a gift from God to be used for the flourishing of all of God's children.

So, if you are a church leader, how do you engage a donor in these absentee conversations? It begins with imagination. Craig Dykstra, former senior vice president for the Religion Division at Lilly Endowment, describes "pastoral imagination" as: "The capacity good pastors have to enter many diverse situations and see what is going on through the eyes of faith. This way of seeing and interpreting shapes what the pastor thinks and does and how she or he responds to people in gestures, words and actions. It functions as a kind of internal gyroscope, guiding pastoral leaders in and through every crevice of their life and work."[16]

Sit down, close your eyes, grab hold of your imagination and picture yourself sitting at your donor's kitchen table. Pull an empty chair up to that table and imagine yourself overhearing everything that is said. What do you hear? What do you think your donors talk about when you're not present? How do they talk about their church and their giving? What words do they use? What emotions do they portray? How then, can you set the table for the conversation your partners will have with themselves? What issues and questions matter to them?

As I have listened to donors talk about their giving, I have concluded that five table-setting issues touch givers' hearts and shape their charitable giving decisions.

1. The donor's perception of an institution's leaders. How do leaders represent the institutions they serve?
2. Clarity as to the institution's mission and vision. Donors want to know what God has called you to be and do and how you do what you do.
3. Organizational readiness. Is everyone on board with all the key players ready to lead the fundraising charge? Donors are reticent to support marginal or failing campaigns.
4. Faith and religious beliefs. In what ways do donors see their giving to the church as giving to God?
5. The congregation's practice of fundraising. Is the annual fundraising program a joyful practice or a tiresome dirge?

The focus of this book is on these five oft-neglected issues. Religious fundraising is a calling and a ministry. Behind every successful church stewardship campaign sit years of work, prayer and spiritual formation. While fundraising gimmicks may entice, they have a short shelf life. It is not my intent to demean the sacredness of fundraising by providing you with quick fixes or novel practices. My hope and prayer are that this book will provide you with a roadmap leading to your donors' giving tables.

# TABLE TALK

## For Personal Reflection

- Where and when do you engage in thoughtful conversation relative to your charitable giving?
- When you reflect on your charitable giving, when and why have you found joy in making a gift?

## For Group Reflection & Conversation

- In what ways is the paradigm shift in charitable giving described in this chapter affecting or reshaping giving in your congregation?
- I listed seven bullet points (p. 9) that describe the distinct ways the new paradigm offers life-changing hope to congregations. Which of these strike you as potentially pertinent to your congregation?

## Action Steps

- As you read this introductory chapter, what did you find most important and meaningful? Make a list of the issues you may need to address as a congregation.

---

[1] "2014 U.S. Trust Study of High Net Worth Philanthropy," 61 percent of married people make their charitable giving decision together. Another 20 percent confer with their spouse or partner before making their own decision.

[2] Martin Luther, *Table Talk*, "Luther's Works," Vol. 54, p. ix.

[3] "NextGenDonors: Respecting Legacy, Revolutionizing Philanthropy," Johnson Center at Grand Valley State, 2013.

[4] George McCully, *Philanthropy Reconsidered.*

[5] Giving USA Foundation,"Giving USA 2016," Indiana University.

[6] Giving USA Foundation, "Giving USA 2017," Indiana University.

[7] "The Philanthropy Outlook 2017-2019," Lilly Family School of Philanthropy, January, 2017.

8 Christopher Scheitle, *Beyond the Congregations: The World of Christian Nonprofits.* National Center for Charitable Statistics. (NCCS) Database for the Urban Institute.

9 Connected to Give, "Faith Communities, 2013."

10 Karl Zinsmeister, "How Philanthropy Fuels American Success," The Philanthropy Roundtable, 1/11/16.

11 McCully, p. 58.

12 "How Donors Choose Charities," The Centre for Philanthropy, University of Kent, 2010.

13 Kelly S. Johnson, *The Fear of Beggars.* Mary J. Oates, *The Catholic Philanthropic Tradition.*

14 Patricia Snell, Brandon Vaidyanathan, "Motivations for and Obstacles to Religious Financial Giving," Sociology of Religion, 2011, Volume 72, Issue 2.

15 Amy Sherman, "Directions in Women's Giving, 2012," Sagamore Institute, 2012.

16 Craig Dykstra, "Cultivating Thriving Communities of Change," Lake Lecture, Lake Institute on Faith & Giving, 2004.

# (2)

## LEADERS AS NURSING MOTHERS

*"The first responsibility of a leader is to define reality. The last is to say thank you."[1]*
*Max DePree*

It was one of those "Aha" moments. I was meeting with a group of lay people representing ten congregations whose pastors had been part of a seminar on "Faith, Money & Giving." An unexpected candor framed the conversation because the pastors weren't present. Participants were free to tell it as they saw it relative to their church and money. The eagerness with which they talked about faith and giving caught me by surprise. They were also curious: Why were church leaders shy and silent when it came to talking about money matters? Why did their leaders only talk about money relative to fundraising? And why—when they did talk about issues related to money—were they cautious and apologetic?

What were these lay men and women looking for from their leaders? They were seeking spiritual partners to converse with as they pondered real life financial issues. They yearned for fellow travelers who could serve as guides and walk beside them as they navigated the challenges of life and money. Then it happened. A team member from one congregation spoke up, saying, "We have that kind of leader. Our new pastor does that. She talks about money as Jesus talked about money and how it relates to everyday life. And last year our giving went up 35 percent." The room went silent. Everyone wanted details.

Effective religious fundraising begins with leadership. Clergy are the public face for most congregations. People give to people—to people they trust and to institutions and leaders who are making a difference.

# 61%

donors say "name recognition trumps
impact" when it comes to giving
decisions[2]

Leaders incite trust when they address real life issues and connect giving to mission. In a money-oriented culture, how leaders talk about money matters. In every congregation-based research project I monitored, I found leadership—lay as well as clergy—to be the key to a fiscally generous and healthy congregation. Here's an example.

Kelly was the new associate pastor in a Lutheran congregation that traditionally held a food and clothing drive each year at Thanksgiving. Kelly's first assignment was to lead this mission project as the congregation sleepily filled a hundred or so food and clothing bags each year. Kelly had a larger vision that she dynamically shared one Sunday in her homily. She envisioned congregation members putting their arms around the needy in their neighborhood and witnessing to the reality that Jesus was alive and present in their town. She then challenged them to fill not one hundred bags of food and clothing but five hundred. Her personal enthusiasm ignited a contagion that captured the imagination and spread like wildfire through the congregation.

After church that Sunday, a six-year-old boy sitting at the kitchen table with his parents asked what he could do. The family decided to create "Kids Kits" that would include toothpaste, toothbrushes, soap, shampoo and lotion for the church's related food pantry. Their dentist heard of the project and donated four cases of dental supplies. The day following the sermon a woman came to Kelly's office and gave her an envelope she had been saving for such a moment containing $1,000 in small bills with the charge to "fan the fire." A week or so later the high school youth group, feeling

> **"Leaders are the midwives of a congregation's vision."**

neglected, decided they would try to fill the five hundred bags themselves. The final congregational tally was 870 bags of food and clothing plus 97 "Kids Kits" in addition to the donation from the dentist.

"I never thought it would be so simple," Kelly wrote, summarizing the project. "It started with a vision and an invite, then came the challenge that exploded into a movement. What did I learn? Building a giving culture begins where a need exists that everyone can buy into and claim as their own."

Why was Kelly's project so successful? In a word, Kelly was authentic. Intuitively she grasped the limitations of the old hierarchical top-down management style. Givers want to be respected and listened to as partners, having a voice in what is happening. In addition to money, donors bring other gifts to the giving table: professional expertise, network connections and institutional wisdom. While a leader may have good intentions and a legitimate cause, an "I'll-tell-you-what-to-do approach" seldom inspires. By contrast, when donors are part of the conversation, their giving becomes expansive and personal. When people give, regardless of the size of the gift, they are giving part of themselves.

What does Kelly's story tell us about the relationship between leadership and effective fundraising? What are the characteristics that capture givers' imagination and touch their hearts?

Leadership has to do with style, character and interpersonal moxie. Donors are moved by leaders who:

- Model a leadership style that is innovative and institution-serving, not self-serving. Kelly saw her congregation for what it could be, not for what it had been. She took a sleepy annual mission project and infused new vision and urgency.
- Mirror a world to which they want to belong. Leaders inspire their givers by the manner in which they embody and articulate the vision and mission of the cause they represent. Kelly embraced her

assignment with a passion that was personal and a zest that became contagious.

- Embrace fundraising as a ministry rather than a duty. Kelly saw her assignment as a way her congregation could wrap God's arms around its neighborhood community. More importantly, her enthusiastic spirit, coupled with her personal openness, transformed her into a trusted conversation partner. Her parishioners saw her as someone with whom they could discuss issues related to faith, money and giving.

## Effective religious fundraisers are institution-serving.

Leaders do not do what they do for personal gain or glory. Business guru Jim Collins describes such leaders as:

*"People who are ambitious first and foremost for the cause, the movement, the mission, the work...and people who will do whatever it takes to make good on that ambition."* [3]

Such leaders have mastered the fine art of navigating the institutional and human networks that shape the life of every congregation. They are adept at building bridges and brokering relationships in their pursuit of a mission and vision that is larger than any one person. Their charisma is framed in humility and in their ability to share a story that is contagious, a story they embody in their own life and living. They do not so much ask for money as they invite people to be part of what God is about in the neighborhood.

## Effective religious fundraisers are dream-makers!

Their focus is missional! They are women and men out to change their neighborhoods. They infuse tired programs with new vision and relevance. Their fundraising focus is not on getting enough money to survive another year but on the vision they have for their congregation's tomorrow. When they talk about money, they are aspirational because they see money as a tool to use for redemptive purposes. They tell stories of changed lives. They are we, not I, people. They invite collaboration as they focus on questions like: What is God calling us to do? What are the mission opportunities sitting on the doorstep of our congregation? They fundraise to enhance God's kingdom, not to meet a budget or fan their personal egos.

## Effective religious fundraisers view fundraising as ministry.

They embrace stewardship as a spiritual practice. Money, as they see it, is a gift of God, not something intrinsically evil. They make money-talk—how we acquire it, manage it, spend it—a staple in their teaching and preaching. They are aware of the giving patterns of their members and attendees and understand this to be part of pastoral care, a sacred trust. Consequently, when it comes to making the "ask" or "appeal" for money, they are not apologetic. What is the secret to their audacity? They have made a pastorally enriching discovery: Fundraising becomes a joy rather than a chore when viewed as ministry. It is in their giving that people often find their calling.

A participant in one of our seminars told me a memorable story. As she was about to board a plane to fly to a seminar in Indianapolis, she ran into the CEO of the local United Way. He inquired as to where she was going; she told him that she was attending a seminar on religious fundraising. "Goodness me," he responded. "If you religious people ever get smart about fundraising, the rest of us may be in trouble."

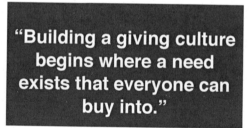

"Building a giving culture begins where a need exists that everyone can buy into."

Why do many clergy find fundraising to be distasteful? A disproportionate number have a jaundiced view of money and people of wealth. I once asked a group of pastors to describe in one word their feelings when working with persons of wealth in their congregation. One team of four pastors wrote down these words: Comfortable, uncomfortable, scared, pissed off. I then listened as each pastor unpacked the personal history behind their word.

The pastor who wrote "comfortable" had majored in economics and earned an MBA before going to seminary. The pastor who wrote "uncomfortable" had never had a course in economics or administration and did not know how to read a financial spread sheet. Keeping money-talk and people of wealth at bay was her way of shielding her financial ignorance. "Scared" described a pastor who had grown up in a modest social-economic setting and seldom had the opportunity to interact with persons of wealth. "Pissed off" reflected a pastor who carried within his soul the scars of economic hurt and personal injustice. His experience left him suspicious and judgmental of anyone with money. Whatever the reason, when a pastor views money as evil or people with money as suspect, fundraising becomes a violation of the conscience rather than a joyful calling.

What do these stories tell us about clergy and fundraising? Frequently, a deep discomfort muddies the way in which clergy perceive money and fundraising, and for a very good reason. Many pastors have told me that as they look at the annual stewardship program in their congregation, it has but one unsettling purpose: to raise the money to pay their salary. This leaves them understandably skittish as to the role they should play in the annual fundraising event. Others confess that they shy away from fundraising because their own finances are in embarrassing disarray as they struggle to provide for their family on a modest income.[4] Some participate, but begrudgingly, and their dour presence is like a virus infecting the fundraising esprit de corps. Yet here is an arresting irony. In our work with hundreds of congregations we discovered this relative to the giving of clergy.

# top 10%

**clergy are usually among the most generous givers in the congregations they serve**

Clergy are generous givers! They just don't like to talk about money or giving—and their silence becomes their Achilles' heel.

The challenge of money-talk in the church is more than a pastoral or leadership issue, it is also a congregational issue. For example, take clergy salaries. It is true, the largest piece of the annual congregational budget usually goes to staff salaries. So, congregations can be irritably hush-hush when it comes to fundraising. In the Hebrew Scriptures, however, it was not considered to be "unspiritual" to talk about clergy salaries. It was the responsibility of the faith community to see that clergy were fairly remunerated. (See Numbers 18, Deuteronomy 18, 2 Chronicles 31) Today, many congregations are reticent to face up to this reality for a variety of reasons. Donors can be prickly, church committees mulish, congregational politics divisive and ego-centric personalities challenging. Consequently, silence rules and the taboo of money-talk in the church lives on.

There is no one-stop turnkey answer to the fiscal challenges facing many congregations. In many ways congregations are like elephants—cumbersome, with short attention spans and a herd instinct. Changing the giving culture of an institution is like teaching an elephant to dance; it requires patience and a long view of ministry. That said, as my Muslim friend and renowned interfaith leader Eboo Patel has wisely observed, "People change when they are taught by people whom they find reliable and inspiring."[5]

> "The first duty of a Christian leader is to provide a Christian perspective for people who want to lead faithful lives."
> Scott Cormode

Is there a metaphor that captures the leadership style for effective religious fundraising? The Bible offers a striking metaphor to describe Moses as leader: "Nursing Mother." (Numbers 11:12) Initially Moses sees this to be a belittling metaphor. He is beside himself; what has Yahweh called him to do? The Hebrew people are contentious and complaining, with the Exodus looming as a colossal failure. Disgruntled, Moses mockingly asks: "Am I their mother? Am I called to carry them in my arms like a nursing mother...all the way to the Promised Land?" In the vexing silence that follows, it is as if Yahweh says, "Yes, Moses; that is what you are, a nursing mother!"

As nursing mother, Moses came to see the Hebrew people not for what they were as slaves and bricklayers but for what they could become.[6] He was God's stand-in to clarify a vision for a people who had differing perceptions as to what that vision meant. His task was to inspire commitment and unify opposing points of view. As nursing mother, Moses modeled superb parenting skills as he endured his people's childish naiveté, abided their adolescent rebelliousness and placated their senilities. At times the task pulled Moses apart, but he persisted, driven by his vision of the Promised Land. As the Hebrew people plodded toward the Promised Land, Moses enabled them to embrace the vision and celebrate a new identity. In the end, this style of leadership was transformational.

The road was long and meandering, but Moses did lead the Hebrews to the river's edge of the Promised Land. He lived true to his calling; it was his sense of vision that made the difference. It is said that God moves slowly so wise leaders take the long view in mothering the congregations they nurse. Leaders as nursing mothers enable congregations to believe in themselves.

How do leaders do that? Louise is the pastor of an African-American congregation about to celebrate its fiftieth anniversary. Congregation members want to raise $100,000 as part of their celebration. However, the congregation struggles to meet its annual budget and it has been more than thirty years since they have had a successful fundraising campaign. Over time, self-doubt blurred their vision and dampened their enthusiasm. Louise's challenge was to change the way her congregation saw itself; from a "can't-do" to a "can-do" people of God.

Louise began small. First, she met with a group of three women she describes as "spiritually-mature and passionate for building up the body of Christ." Together, they talked and prayed before designing a mini-campaign to, as they put it, "test the waters." They focused on a need that was simple and obvious; something everyone could embrace. The carpet in the chapel was threadbare, there was also a strong desire to embrace a more contemporary musical style in their worship. The purpose of their project was to raise $16,000 to install new carpet and purchase the equipment needed as the congregation transitioned to a new style of worship. They presented their idea to their Church Council. The Church Council unanimously endorsed the plan and a Giving Ministry team was created to oversee the campaign. In December they rolled out a "Christmas Gift to the Church" program in which they raised $17,000 in gifts and pledges. Easter Sunday, 2016, they celebrated the resurrection with newly installed carpet and worship equipment.

In summarizing her experience as a nursing mother, Louise wrote: "I've discovered that I like talking about money. I've also learned a lot about leadership. I've learned how to ask questions and engage lay leaders and large givers in conversation. As a leadership team we grew closer and grew as leaders. Together we navigated our system without discord. Nearly all of our members and attendees participated. Best of all, we're now positioned to kick off our fiftieth anniversary celebration with joy and confidence."

Leaders both cradle and crystalize their congregation's vision. In their public and private conversations, they focus not on what is but what can be as they paint inviting pictures of their congregation's tomorrow. They then live and embody that vision in all they do. They pursue their vision one step at a time and pause to celebrate each new success before moving ahead. It's the long view of Christian discipleship that unleashes generous giving.

People give generously when they are inspired by a vision that inflames their hearts and leaders who embody that vision in their life and ministry. My friend Jim describes himself as "a begrudging church giver." Recently he told me that he has put the church in his will and now gives with joy. "What happened?" I asked. Jim replied, "We have a pastor who is relational, trustworthy and visionary. He lives what he says."

As the old proverb warns: "Where there is no vision—when people can't see what God is doing—they stumble over themselves and perish." (Proverbs 29:18)

# TABLE TALK

## For Personal Reflection

- What are some of the challenges you face in your congregation when it comes to fundraising and money-talk?

## For Group Reflection & Conversation

- What are three changes that you believe would be most helpful in your congregation's approach to fundraising?

## Action Steps

- List the issues relative to money, mission and fundraising you might address as leaders in your congregation.
- Discuss the ways by which you as a leadership team - clergy and laity - might begin to address these issues.

---

[1] Max DePree, *Leadership is an Art.*

[2] "Money for Good," 2015.

[3] Jim Collins, *Good to Great and the Social Sectors.*

[4] "Pay Scale 2017," The median clergy salary is listed as $51,352.

[5] Eboo Patel. *Interfaith Leadership*, p. 12.

[6] Aaron Wildavsky, *The Nursing Father. Moses as a Political Leader*, p.57ff.

# (3)

## WHO ARE YOU? WHAT HAVE YOU BEEN CALLED TO BE AND DO?

*"Nonprofit institutions are human change agents. Their product is a changed human life altogether."[1]*
*Peter Drucker*

Clarity as to who you are and what you do as a congregation lays the foundation for effective religious fundraising. A mission that is purpose-driven and visionary stirs donors' hearts and captures their imagination. Clarity in calling sets gung-ho congregations apart from ho-hum congregations.

Our congregation was growing and we needed more space. Our governing board gave us the green light to explore our options. We hired an architect to draw up preliminary plans for a major building addition. Our last step was to engage a fundraising consultant to guide us on our journey. Don was the gentle, but candid, truth teller who became my trusted friend and mentor as he walked beside me, taking the fear out of fundraising. Don first conducted a feasibility study in which he interviewed people who had the fiscal capacity to become our major donors. Then came our comeuppance. We thought we were ready to charge ahead when Don's report snapped our heads back like a big yellow caution sign blocking the road. While our donors loved us, they failed to see the need for a building expansion and questioned its relevance to our mission.

Detours are commonplace in fundraising campaigns; however, they need not derail a campaign. Truth be told, fundraising detours are often redemptive. They make table talk public as they give rise to overlooked questions and issues which, when addressed, become the building blocks for a successful campaign. So we listened to Don and learned from him. We did our homework; we addressed the issues and answered the questions. The result: We met our goal and dedicated the new addition later than anticipated but debt free. While detours may alter the timeline of a fundraising initiative, they can be providential gifts to embrace.

Where had we gone awry? In a sentence, we had failed to make our case for support. We thought the need was obvious and assumed that all we had to do was ask and people would give. In our naiveté we unwittingly ignored a basic fundraising principle: Giving is personal, and personal investments are seldom made willy-nilly!

> "The purpose of a fundraising case statement is to answer questions: What do you do? Who do you do it for? What's the impact?"

When people give something, they are giving away part of who they are; be it money, an idea, a skill or a networking connection. People give to friends and causes they believe in. They give to needs that are personally compelling and to programs worthy of support. Clarity as to need, mission and vision is pivotal to any successful fundraising effort. Clarity as to why you do what you do provides donors a lens through which to assess and focus their giving.

Why is clarity imperative? Most donors are pressed with more giving opportunities than they can support. Thoughtful donors ask questions. Questions like: "What do you do?" "Who do you do it for?" "What's the impact of what you are doing?" "Why do you need more money to do what you do?". The purpose of a fundraising case statement is to answer such questions. The more informed the donor is as to the mission of an organization, the more generous they are in their giving.[2] Good case statements inform and educate giving partners. They are succinct; crafted to quickly get to the point and capture the heart and mind of the prospective donor. Everything you do should be seen through the lens of your mission.

Givers motivated by faith ask additional and even more important institutional questions: "Who are you? Why do you do what you do?" Those were the questions a group of religious priests put to John the Baptist and they were the questions Pilate asked Jesus. (John 1:19ff; 18:33ff) They are questions demanding religious answers because people of faith want to connect God to their giving.

In many congregations, fundraising had been trivialized and reduced to little more than a mimicry of secular fundraising practices. Religious fundraising is unique in that it gives you an opportunity to talk about God as you invite people to partner with you in a specific ministry or mission. Religiously motivated donors want to know how, by what you do, you serve as Christ's hands and feet in a hurting world. The world needs doctors and teachers and plumbers and techies, but why does the neighborhood need your church? Never assume that the people sitting in your pews know the answer to that question, so be clear as to what motivates you as a congregation to do what you do!

Some time ago this headline from a New York Times editorial made me sit up straight: "Jen Shang Understands the Power of Prayer – to Open Wallets!"[3] Jen Shang is a professor of philanthropic psychology at Indiana University and Plymouth University in England. In her research she has discovered prayer and religious convictions to be powerful motivating factors as donors view their gifts as expressions of who they are and what they believe.[4] Simply put, it is in their giving that donors witness to their faith.

Most of us will not be privileged to personally sit at our donors' tables. Yet our presence hovers incognito in donors' minds as they ponder their giving. The manner in which a congregation describes itself and carries out its mission makes us silent partners in the conversation. One congregation I served described its mission with this memorable umbrella phrase: "We exist to put God's arms around our city and God's world." As I watched that congregation live out its mission with exuberance, I learned a life-changing lesson. In religious fundraising, money follows mission. Why and how we do what we do imprints donors' minds.

> "The story of a changed life puts a human face on the dry bones of a mission or ministry."

Sadly, congregations are not particularly adept in addressing donors' questions. Why is this? Many are ignorant as to the questions donors ask. Others are too modest to flag or publicly headline the impact their ministry is making. Some incredulously dismiss fundraising as child's play, naively believing that they need do nothing as "the Lord will provide." Congregations are also vulnerable to what I call Saint Paul's disease. In a misread of Paul's testimony that he "became all things to all people" (1 Corinthians 9:22), they lose themselves in a maze of activities that mask any identity-defining purpose. So donors wonder what it is that sets a congregation's mission apart from the good work of the secular nonprofit down the street. Paul's flexibility and adaptability was driven by an identity-defining purpose: "Everything I do I do for the sake of the gospel."

The question "what sets you apart?" is challenging because it unleashes a string of soul-searching issues for congregations to ponder.

- On what do you base your congregational identity? Is it your denominational heritage, your theology, your geographical location, the demographics of your congregation?
- What do you believe God is calling you to do and be?
- Is the purpose of your annual fundraising program to raise just enough money to get you through another year or is it to share a vision and invite people to join you in your mission?
- In what ways does your fundraising program reflect your congregation's vision of its tomorrow?

The more indifferent or negligent you are as to the core reason for your existence, the less money you will raise.

Congregations that are robustly innovative spark their donors' imaginations.

What captures donors' hearts and minds? (1) Stories that are aspirational and informational. (2) Timely new ventures that reflect timeless values. (3) Communications that are data-driven yet personal and donor-friendly.

## Stories should be both aspirational and informational.

Generous givers love to hear stories of difference-makers and stories of changed lives because they yearn for hope. Hope stretches the contours of our hearts and ultimately our checkbooks. A good story has an emotional frame; it captures a giver's heart because it is the compelling story of a life transformed by the ministry of the congregation. It is a story told with a passion that connects the donor to the mission of the church as it answers the giver's "so what?" question. It's the story of a changed life that puts a human face on the dry bones of a mission or ministry.

Nonprofit institutions—including congregations—are human change agents. In the words of the late management guru Peter Drucker, "their product is a changed human life altogether."[5] Jesus had a knack for answering questions by telling transformational stories to make his case. A good story breathes life into the otherwise dollar blur of a budget.

In one of our seminars, John began his story with these riveting words: "My ministry takes place at the abandoned intersections of life where live the homeless, the hungry, the forgotten of our city." Instantly John had our attention. Then, as we leaned forward, he lost us as he proceeded to describe ad nauseam the programs offered through his organization. When he had finished I asked him if he had a story he might tell to humanize his ministry. He replied, "Yes, but I'm afraid I'll cry." "John," I replied, "in storytelling, tears are luminous." He then proceeded to tell the story of a homeless man who stumbled into his mission in need of food and medical care. At the end of a long afternoon when the man was about to leave following a visit to the medical clinic he paused saying: "How can I thank you? Can I give you a hug? I haven't hugged anyone in years." And tears filled the eyes of all of us in the room as John became for us Christ's healing and caring presence.

Stories that lead with emotion are both aspirational and informational. They bring information that touches the heart. A good story does more; it is a key that unlocks the door to what my friend Henry Freeman calls that "sacred space." A sacred space is a place to which we only admit those we trust, people with whom we have a relationship. It's a self-revealing space that becomes sacred when a story we hear triggers an "aha!" moment linking us to our own story, who we are and the dreams we yearn to build. It is "in telling and listening to stories that we connect with the world around us."[6]

The philosopher Alasdair MacIntyre writes: "We humans are essentially story-telling animals...I can only answer the question 'What am I to do?' if I can answer the prior question to what story or stories do I find myself to be a part?"[7]

**Timely new ventures should reflect timeless values.**

The words "timely" and "timeless" are the bridge builders connecting the emergent new with the resilient old in congregational life. Change is part of the stuff of ministry when congregations strive to remain relevant in our transient world. While change may be threatening, it need not be divisive. Change becomes polarizing and destructive when it forces people into camps of "this vs. that" or "we vs. they." Timelessness happens when old values and identity-defining callings give birth to new missions and culturally relevant programs.

Effective change is anchored in congregational values that are timeless. Values that are life-giving shape a congregations sense of calling. That said, the journey from timeless values to timely new ventures can be challenging. In his book *How Your Congregation Learns,* Tim Shapiro describes this journey as an "exodus" potholed with "aha moments" as a congregation explores new terrain, acquires new skills, embraces new behaviors and christens a dream.[8]

Why do people resist change? Because they associate change with the loss of practices precious to them. When it comes to money and giving, in many congregations resistance to change is generational. Programs and giving practices that address the needs and desires of one generation may well be alien to the practices and programs of another generation. The prewar generation—my generation—is particularly wary of changes rooted in technology; online giving being a prime example. Older people unfamiliar with technology fear that online giving will end the Sunday offering ritual and foreclose the use of their sacred offering envelopes. Millennials, people born from 1985-2000, don't use envelopes. Their giving is spontaneous, fueled by their passion for a mission or cause. The internet is their pulpit and newspaper. They learn, interact and give primarily via digital technology such as websites, social media, mobile platforms.[9] Lost to my generation is the fact that online giving is a timely investment in their congregation's tomorrow as Millennials are the largest generation in the history of the United States.[10]

How then might a congregation address this fear of loss mingled with its resistance to change? Scott Cormode, my teaching colleague and Hugh DePree Professor of Leadership Development at Fuller Theological Seminary, suggests two words: "innovation" and "improvisation." Both words have something to do with a congregation's willingness to tinker with but not abandon its inherited mission and calling.

Innovation begins with a commitment to speak in such a way as to gain the attention of a new audience. Tinkerers are innovators who seek to map ways in which a congregation can reinvent itself while remaining true to its calling.[11] In the theater, the first rule of "improv" is listening. This means listening to what is said, observing what is happening around you, then adding new insights or new information to the conversation.[12] Innovation and improvisation are the looms weaving together the past and the present as they recycle timeless values with timely new initiatives.

Joe is the executive pastor in a large Baptist church with what he calls a "five- bucket" approach to fundraising. People may give to five separate budgets: an operations budget, a mission budget, a building fund, a debt-retirement budget, a special offering budget. While the congregation has a history of 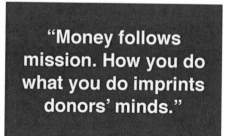 generous giving and good business management, the "five-bucket" approach is no longer working. People are increasingly giving to those buckets that reflect their interests, saddling Joe's congregation with a

"Money follows mission. How you do what you do imprints donors' minds."

diminished operations budget that no longer can meet the day-to-day cost of running the church. So, the leadership of the church revisited their giving and fundraising practices and concluded that a unified budget would better serve their needs than the "five-bucket" approach. They also determined that it was best for them to change and base their budget on the calendar year rather than the congregational program year. These were big, dramatic changes that left the church's governing board anxious as to how the congregation would respond.

With thoughtful care the leaders designed a seven-step, six-month transition program to test the validity of the change while addressing the questions buzzing through the church.

1. First, they engaged more than five hundred members in personal dialogue.
2. The data they collected from the member conversations was given to a committee of fifty people who were responsible for overseeing the decision-making process.
3. They created a personalized mailing program for each member household detailing their giving patterns.
4. They communicated, communicated, communicated! Via a marketing video they informed the congregation as to the fiscal challenge they were addressing. To dramatize the challenge they created an on-site infographic of water flowing into five buckets.
5. The senior pastor became the chief communicator. He held ten unified budget hearings and regularly informed the congregation from the pulpit and via the weekly newsletter as to what was happening.
6. They used the transition period to explore new fundraising opportunities.
7. The six-month gap between the current program year and the calendar year served as a time to pilot and experiment with a unified budget. Based on their "five-bucket" model, they needed to raise $2.5 million to fund this gap period.

Were they successful? The fundraising goal for their gap unified budget was $2.5 million; they raised $2.75 million.

## Donor-friendly communications are personal and data-driven.

Effective case statements are donor-friendly and data-driven, speaking to both the head and the heart. In making the case for change or when raising money to launch a new initiative, data matter. Good data answer the "so what" questions: "Is this new venture warranted and necessary? If we change, will we get what we want? Why do we need more money to run this program?" Data that are research-driven and people-focused speak to the reservations pinching a donor's mind. Why was Joe successful? His team collected giving data covering seven years for each member. The five hundred people they interviewed became their teachers.

Data can also highlight those fundraising issues needing attention. A Texas congregation had an extraordinarily high percentage of its members who made an annual pledge. Yet, they experienced a significant budget deficit at the end of each fiscal year. Why this deficit? Fifty percent of those households making a pledge failed to pay their pledge in full.

A large mission program with an international focus on children thought it was swimming in success because of the number of new donors signing on each year. Then it took a hard look at its data. While they were growing new partners and gaining more money each year, they also were losing partners and money each year: 4,000 lost donors dating back to 2010.

In the nonprofit world, the number of new donors and dollars gained in a year is offset by the number of donors and dollars lost.

**$92**

**amount of money lost per $100 gained in
2014 from lapsed or lost donors[13]**

Data are revelatory, identifying realities that must be addressed.

Congregations seldom receive the recognition they deserve for the difference they make via their programs and services. Taking the time to unearth data can be a revolutionary game changer for donors. In a recent study of more than a hundred urban congregations in Philadelphia, Chicago and Fort Worth, Dr. Ram Cnaan, director of the Program for Religion and Social Policy Research at the University of Pennsylvania, found the economic impact—the "halo effect"—of these congregations to be on average $1.7 million annually.[14] To a congregation, be it large or small, the economic impact of a ministry or outreach program in its neighborhood far exceeded the dollar expenditure listed in the budget.

How do organizations collect this kind of information? In determining the economic or "halo effect" of a program:[15]

- Focus on one particular program or outreach ministry.
- Use the hourly minimum wage to determine the dollar value of those who serve as volunteers in the program.
- Place a dollar value on the type of services provided: the cost per meal for a hot meal program, the cost for a bag of groceries from a food pantry, the cost of a night's lodging to shelter the homeless, the cost of a gift contributed to a program, the economic value of a marriage saved.
- Add these numbers together to assess the "halo effect."

Good data both inform and boggle givers' minds, enabling them to see God at work in their neighborhood in ways beyond their expectations.

Peter is the rector of a thriving Episcopal congregation. He was curious; everyone takes Sunday school for granted, but what was the actual yearly cost of a Sunday school class to his parish? He did his research; the cost was $700 per child, or about $10,000 per class. That information was transformative; it personalized the congregation's annual stewardship program and giving reached a new level.

Gary, the new pastor of a smaller Presbyterian congregation in a "no growth" community, developed a twelve-question survey to gather information relative to the members of his congregation. His goal was to uncover the dreams and silent longings of his congregants' hearts. He discovered that the congregation had one defining purpose: to fellowship with and care for each other, as a family of faith, and to serve their community. That learning resulted in a new mission statement

> "Congregations that are robustly innovative spark their donors' imagination."

which was turned into a public relations flyer that was posted around town in the local Starbucks and the public library. Gary then developed a series of sermons around the new mission statement. The creation of a collaborative mission statement blessed the congregation with an identity-defining purpose that resulted in a 15 percent increase in annual giving.

Ann serves a mid-size, county-seat church where the status-quo defines the congregation. The congregation needed to replace its fraying hymnbooks, but the $18,000 cost was daunting. Church music can also be contentious. The proposed hymnal instantly became a flashpoint of controversy as it included contemporary as well as traditional hymns. Ann, sensing the divide to be generational as well as musical, took time to engage people in one-on-one conversations as to their musical likes and dislikes. She then formed a committee composed of people mirroring all sides of the debate. She played the role of listening moderator. She hosted dessert coffees and intentionally engaged in conversation with individuals from three formal social networks in the congregation. Sometime later she learned of an informal network of retired men opposed to the new hymnbook, who met daily on the town square for coffee. So one day she just happened to "pop in" and joined their conversation. As she listened to the various groups express their fears and reservations as well as their loves and joys, attitudes began to change and a small miracle happened. The congregation became aware as to what hymns had deep meaning for people and why. When the vote for the new hymnals was taken, it was virtually unanimous—and the money was there.

A convincing fundraising case statement weaves together aspirational stories and relevant data in such a way as to personalize support for ministries old and new. But, beware, this is not a task to achieve on a whim and in a whisk. Making your fundraising case is like farming and gardening. You plant and sow, weed and water, plow and fertilize. You wait, as St. Paul noted long ago, but with this magnificent difference: "It happens to be God's field in which we are working...and it is God who makes things grow." (I Corinthians 3:7)

What is fundraising? It is a report card as to the clarity of your vision and the effectiveness of your mission as seen through the eyes of your giving partners as they look back from their conversation tables.

# TABLE TALK

## For Personal Reflection

- Take a moment and reflect on the programs and ministries of your congregation. What is special or unique about your church? Try to describe in one or two sentences what you see your congregation called to be and do.

## For Group Reflection & Conversation

- Share with each other your thoughts on the personal reflection question.
- If your congregation has a mission statement, in what ways does your conversation resonate with your mission statement?
- Step back and reflect on who you are and what you do, then look ahead to your congregation's tomorrow. What gives you joy? What do you see as your challenges?

## Action Steps

- Analyze one mission or ministry of your congregation and see if you can assess the "halo effect" of that mission to share with your congregation.
- Visit with the leaders of that mission or ministry and collect a story or two to share with your congregation of a life changed because of that program

---

[1] Peter Drucker, *Managing the Non-Profit Organization: Principles and Practices.*

[2] U.S. Trust, "Study of High Net Worth Philanthropy," 2016.

[3] David Wallis, The New York Times, November 8, 2012.

[4] Adrian Sargent & Jen Shang: *Fundraising Principles and Practice*, Chapter 4.

[5] Peter Drucker.

[6] Henry Freeman, *Unlacing the Heart, p.3.*

7 Alasdair MacIntyre, *After Virtue*, p. 216.

8 Tim Shapiro, *How Your Congregation Learns*.

9 "The Millennial Impact Report Retrospective: Five Years of Trends," November, 2016.

10 The Colloquy, February, 2017, An interview with Frank Yamada, newly appointed CEO of The Association of Theological Schools.

11 Steven Johnson, "The Genius of the Tinkerer," The Wall Street Journal, 9/25/2010.

12 `David Alger,"First Ten Rules of Improv," Course Handout: Dr. Scott Cormode, Fuller Theological Seminary.

13 "Fundraising Effectiveness Survey Report," Association of Fundraising Professionals and The Urban Institute, 2016.

14 "Sacred Places National Report: The Economic Halo Effect of Historic Sacred Places," 2016.

15 David O'Reilly, "A Study Asks: What's a Church's Economic Worth?" The Philadelphia Inquirer, 2/1/11.

# (4)

## GETTING EVERYONE ONBOARD

*"Trustees must address two issues: the readiness of the board to provide the kind of leadership an organization deserves and the worthiness of the organization to receive the goodwill and gifts it desires."[1]*
*Rebekah Basinger*

It was one of the most successful fundraising projects in human history. You can read all about it in Exodus, chapters 35-36. The Hebrew people were about to build a place for worship. As leader, Moses called the people together and made the case for building the tabernacle. The people then went to their homes to talk about it. The case was so compelling that the response of the people exceeded all expectations and Moses had to send out a STOP THE CAMPAIGN bulletin! What made this fundraising effort so successful? Prior to beginning the fundraising effort, Moses took time to prepare his congregation. He focused on organizational issues and created an esprit de corps that made everyone want to be involved. Everyone had something to bring or do.

Your fundraising case may be clear; now comes this testy question: Are you ready to go public with your fundraising? One word bars the door to a successful fundraising effort—readiness! Is your congregation organizationally ready to fundraise? Are all the key players on board for the venture?

St. Anne's is a growing multi-cultural Catholic parish with two parish church locations and one school. The congregation recently retired a sizable loan, leaving it debt free. Then came a serendipitous offer; the parish was given the opportunity to reclaim a large property that had once housed a girls' boarding school for a dollar-a-month lease with an option to purchase the facility for $1 million to be paid out over twenty years at $50,000 a year. The offer captured the imagination of many in the parish as it would allow St. Anne's to: (1) expand its educational and athletic offerings, (2) extend its social service missions to include the city center location of a historic Catholic property, (3) enable the parish to initiate a new mission focusing on the theater and the arts. Can St. Anne's make a compelling case for the purchase of the property? Is St. Anne's ready to successfully engage in a fundraising campaign?

Delores chaired the task force charged with making the "go or no-go" decision. Their verdict: St. Anne's was not ready to engage in a successful fundraising project for two reasons.

> **"One word bars the door to a successful fundraising effort—readiness! Are all the key players onboard?"**

First, money-talk had become a taboo subject at St. Anne's. While Father Daniel, the pastor, was energetic with a passion for missions, he suffered from lockjaw when it came to talking about God and money, giving and fundraising. He viewed fundraising as a secular vice and saw little spiritual about money. Alas, lockjaw can be contagious and in time the stewardship committee at St. Anne's caught the virus. They vetoed an effort to conduct a parish giving survey fearing that it would surface questions regarding fiscal transparency. They discontinued the practice of sending monthly thank you cards to parishioners. Delores and her committee also discovered that most people gave and served more out of a sense of duty than gratitude. As a result, the monthly offertory donations at St. Anne's had spiraled downward as the haunting silence surrounding money and possessions resulted in a congregation of uninformed and lackadaisical givers. Before St. Anne's is ready to embark on a new fundraising initiative, it must learn how to talk about God, money and giving as a Christian practice.

Delores also discovered St. Anne's to be in organizational disarray. The parish organizational chart consisted of thirty-plus committees and subcommittees. While each committee was responsible for coordinating one area of ministry in the parish, fundraising responsibilities were lodged in three different committees. Atop this hierarchal maze sat the parish counsel and executive committee that needed to approve everything. On the surface, St. Anne's appeared to be an inclusive and well-organized parish. Dig deeper and you found a series of programmatic silos or fiefdoms, each interested only in its particular program. Navigating this maze proved to be a nightmare for Delores as the parish suffered from organizational fatigue. St. Anne's was neither ready nor worthy to receive the gifts and goodwill it desired. First there were organizational issues they must address.

I have observed organizational readiness to be the number one deterrent to a successful fundraising program. Fundraising consultant/coach Karla Williams is right on target when she notes that the ability of an institution to engage in effective fundraising turns on three words: attitude, advocacy, action. "Attitude" reflects the ways the governing board and staff members talk about money and fundraising. "Advocacy" reveals the ways an organization's leaders embrace and financially contribute to the mission of the organization. "Action" describes the ways staff and board members engage donors.[2]

For congregations, the question of readiness most frequently raises its dissenting head in three areas: board or governance issues, cultural practices, generational differences.

**Board & Governance Issues**

I have been privileged to serve on numerous faith-based nonprofit boards. All too often I found myself walking away from board meetings well informed as to programs, services and special events but illiterate as to the fiscal wellbeing of the organization. As I walked away I found myself wondering: Were we so flush with money that we had no need to talk about money? Governing boards have a fiduciary responsibility to monitor with prudence the business decisions made on behalf of the institutions they serve. Silence on fiscal matters can breed a kind of ignorance that naively morphs into irresponsible governance. Low expectations of board members usually lead to miserly giving by board members.

How does one assess the readiness of a board to lead a successful fundraising initiative? Here are seven questions I have found to be revelatory.

- Does your institutional vision shape your budget, or is it your annual budget that determines your vision and mission?
- Does the chairperson of your board regularly discuss fiscal issues with the board?
- How aware are you of the financial health of your congregation?
- Does your pastor or board chair actively engage in fundraising?
- Are all the members of your board financial contributors?
- Is an annual contribution a requirement for board service?
- Do board members see themselves as fundraising advocates on behalf of the institution they serve?

JoAnn chairs the governing board of a denominational judicatory. Lorrie is the executive director of a multi-congregation lay chaplaincy ministry serving a network of urban hospitals. Sam is the new pastor of a congregation whose board prohibits the pastor from being involved in anything that has to do with finances. What do these three leaders have in common? Each of them serves an organization facing major fiscal challenges. Each works with a governing board composed of people representing other organizations or program interests. Each has discovered that only a minority of their board members actually contribute financially to the mission they oversee.

Over time JoAnn, Lorrie and Sam orchestrated a major turnaround in their boards' behaviors. How did this transformation come to be? Each addressed board members' duties and responsibilities. JoAnn and Lorrie's boards were largely made up of individuals whose primary roles were to protect the interests of the organization they represented rather than those of the board on which they sat. Sam, while viewed as the pastor/leader of his congregation, was expected to manage well with his financial hand tied behind his back. All three understood that the issues needing to be addressed were governance issues. So their first step was constitutional: to clarify the roles and expectations of board members. Once new bylaw changes were in place, they began to seed the board with new members. Slowly, as the ethos of their boards began to change, their board members came to see themselves as stewards rather than guardians.

How do board members serve and live out their roles? Do they function as stewards of a vision for tomorrow or as guardians of past successes and values? My longtime friend Jim McLennan, who has served on and chaired numerous religious nonprofits as well as corporate boards across the United States, calls it a critical issue.[3] Guardians are anchored to the past and stuck in the status quo; they act to preserve and protect old interests and bygone alliances. Such were the boards JoAnn and Lorrie inherited. Stewards, by contrast, see themselves to be servants of an institutional vision and calling. Their focus is on tomorrow as they harness their institutional resources in such a way as to embrace the new opportunities on their organizations' doorsteps.

JoAnn, Lorrie and Sam redesigned their bylaws and recruited new board members with the understanding that they would serve as active players, not grandstand spectators. As stewards and role models, each board member was expected to make a financial contribution and be engaged in fundraising on behalf of the organization.

Was there pushback? Absolutely! Change threatens, and some board members resigned. However, as the new boards took shape, amazing things began to happen. In one year the giving level on JoAnn's board jumped from 18 percent to 53 percent. Today, all of Lorrie's board members give. Once Sam became aware of the giving patterns in his church, two of his most critical board members had a checkbook conversion and began to give and pledge.

Fred's challenge was different. Fred is the pastor of a nontraditional congregation that meets on the village beach in the summer and in the chapel of a nearby college in the fall and winter. Fred's church, which began as a creative experiment, has blossomed into a growing enterprise providing spiritual guidance for several hundred families. However, as Fred anticipates the future of his congregation and his own retirement, he is facing organizational and sustainability issues he can no longer ignore. Fred, a bred-in-the-bone visionary, depends on his personal charisma to make things happen. So, he set out to design and launch a multi-million-dollar fundraising program when reality smacked him in the face. A friend pulled him aside and reminded him that if people were going to give for his congregation's tomorrow they needed assurance that come tomorrow the congregation would still be there. Fred then

> "Does your governing board function as stewards of a vision for tomorrow or as guardians of past successes and values?"

stepped back and met with lawyers and financial consultants to draft his first set of congregational bylaws, form a board of directors to whom he would be accountable and set up a solid and transparent financial plan. He brought a young minister on board whom he is grooming to be his successor.  Last year Fred called me to say that he was closing in on the successful completion of a $3 million fundraising effort.

**Cultural Practices**

During my ministry I served two very different congregations.  In the 1970s, I was the pastor of a young, dynamic congregation located in a suburban community with a yearly real estate turnover rate of 25 percent. The leadership of the congregation was dominated by entrepreneurial thirty and forty year olds who coveted leading the annual stewardship campaign. Many were managers and salespersons who lived by deadlines, so they usually waited until September to begin their planning before charging ahead with unbridled gusto. They transformed October into a glorious four weeks of "I pledge" buttons, with giving posters plastering the walls of the sanctuary and a large United Way style thermometer dominating the narthex. October concluded with a rousing pledge Sunday and a close to standing-room-only crowd filling the sanctuary. Amazingly, every year the budget grew significantly, outpacing inflation, and I discovered fundraising to be fun.

The next congregation I served was a historic urban congregation dominated by a corporate mindset that was reflective of the business and community leaders sitting in the pews. I quickly learned that a rah-rah approach to stewardship would not dance. In this congregation, stewardship planning was a thoughtful year-round activity that included numerous fundraising events, culminating in a low-key late-fall pledge campaign. Church attendance on Pledge Sunday was usually modest with pledge commitments trickling in through early January as some waited to clarify their annual income while others prepaid their next-year pledge for tax purposes. The focus in this congregation was not on annual fundraising but on the creation of an institutional culture of generosity. Did it work? Indeed, it did! The lay leaders in this congregation were among the best teachers I ever had. For twenty-plus years I sat back as I listened, learned and watched a church budget grow more than five-fold.

Two different congregations, two different cultures, two different approaches to the annual stewardship drive; yet both were successful because they respected their cultural traditions. Respect for the inherent culture of a congregation is pivotal to a congregation's readiness and worthiness to receive the goodwill and gifts it deserves.

Congregational cultures are frequently shaped by ethnic heritages and different ways of talking about God, money and giving. In part, St. Anne's complex organizational structure reflects the merger of two different parish cultures—one Hispanic, the other Anglo.

In Hispanic cultures, giving is quietly familial and punctuated by joyful, action-oriented public fundraising events. In a Hispanic-Pentecostal congregation, the big fundraiser was the annual boxing gala when a boxing ring was placed in the church courtyard. Among those climbing into the ring, amidst rousing cheers to raise money for Jesus, was Pastor Jose whose father had proceeded him as pastor and whose grandfather had been the founding pastor of the congregation. One Protestant Samoan congregation hosted a monthly Friday night family dinner dance at which parents danced with their children while onlookers tossed money on the dance floor for mission.

Historic black congregations focus on tithing as they teach and practice giving. And, unlike most congregations, they make tithing work. Why?

# +25%

**how much more of their discretionary income African-Americans donate than whites[4]**

Because they view tithing as a way of expressing gratitude to God for the gifts of life, hope and grace.

Lian is a third generation Chinese woman active in an Evangelical church with separate English, Cantonese and Mandarin-speaking congregations. She serves as a member of the congregation's mission committee. Her project was to raise money to send several dozen college students to a large young-adult conference. She was ready to launch her fundraising campaign when the elders in her church stopped her cold. They reminded Lian that fundraising was not a cultural value they encouraged. They advised her to respect the wisdom of the board of elderly men guiding the church. While the church was blessed with abundant fiscal resources, all expenditures were to come from the annual church budget that was based on members' weekly tithes and offerings. No other fundraising was permitted. So, Lian stepped back and allowed the tradition of her culture to work its magic. And it did; in due time the mission committee approved the project from money in the existing church budget.

Every congregation is its own unique culture; it has its own subtle rituals and unspoken rules for doing things. The culture of a congregation in turn reflects its identity and shapes its fundraising practices. Disrespect the culture and the status quo fights back; respect the culture and good things happen.[5]

## Generational Differences

The major generational challenge facing many congregations—as we have noted—has to do with the use of technology. Technology threatens in part because it challenges current practices. Technology by definition is "creatively destructive." What is state-of-the-art today is destined to become obsolete tomorrow. In the high-tech world in which we live, change happens at such a fast pace that it is discombobulating for some. For Millennials, on the other hand, change is the norm of life. This is why congregations that want to attract young people must be open to online giving and willing to use social media in telling their story. With this caveat, in embracing a new practice you need not jettison the old.

> "Most congregations are made up of five living generations, five fairly distinct groups of people."

I think of Sammy's experience. When Sammy was hired, his assignment was to design a marketing program to attract younger people to the ministry of a faith-based, social-service agency serving a historic urban area. Sammy's success came to be viewed as an organizational threat. He created and launched via social media a Young Professional Council attracting more than a million followers on Twitter, including a member of the U.S. Congress. Then came pushback from an unanticipated source—the executive director and the board of directors of the organization. The aging leaders saw themselves as institutional guardians of a successful past. They became "dismissive" of the Young Professional Council fearing that its success posed a threat to their more traditional way of doing business. The real problem? Most of the board members had little understanding of social media. They were blind to the fact that in using social media to nurture a new generation of donors they were not altering the time-honored mission of their organization. Rather, they were growing a new cadre of partners and thereby assuring their organization of a vibrant tomorrow.

As part of their research project, a team of young clergy serving in a larger congregation surveyed their Millennial-aged peers to assess their attitudes toward giving. They discovered that:

- Most Millennials did not feel that the congregation needed their money.
- Millennials believed that secular nonprofits were better at telling their story and more fiscally accountable than the church.
- Millennials preferred to serve and support their church by volunteering for mission projects instead of giving money.

These findings reinforce what research tells us about the religious giving of Millennials; they want to be valued for who they are.[6]

- 96% will research an organization before giving.
- They want their gifts to matter and make a difference.
- They volunteer and give because of who they are, not because they have been asked.
- They demand honesty and fiscal accountability.
- They expect their gifts to be used for stated purposes.
- They relish hands-on experiences with the ministries they support.
- They like to have fun raising money and volunteering.

And, it is Millennials who hold the key to your congregation's tomorrow.

Generational and cultural differences aside, people give for different reasons. First, people give to people—people with whom or through whom they have a relationship. Second, people give to address a need, not to meet a budget. Third, people give to say "thank you" for something good that has happened in their life. Finally, people give to programs and missions that mirror their personal values and passions.

**How do congregations respond to this array of challenges?**

Congregations that are sensitive to these cultural and generational realities are robustly innovative and spark their giving partners' imaginations. They are fundraising savvy. In the words of David Odom, director of Leadership

Education at Duke Divinity School, they understand the future of a mission or ministry to be scary "if service is not tied to revenue and the interests of those providing the funding."[7] They are congregations that think long-term. They are vigilant in asking questions that will measure a ministry's effectiveness and illuminate future opportunities. They embrace change with patience and intentionality.

Craig is a second-career Lutheran pastor who spent most of his life as a broker at Chicago's Board of Trade. He is passionate as to the future of the church so he lives with his eyes focused on God's tomorrow. When he learned that the Wednesday night before Thanksgiving was one of the busiest nights of the year for pubs and taverns, his entrepreneurial instincts kicked in. Working with two Lutheran congregations and a willing tavern owner, he designed a program called "Cover Charge for Charity." On the Wednesday before Thanksgiving, the monies collected as a cover charge would be designated for a local charity. Not only was the program a success with people lined up to get in, but today there exists in that tavern what Craig calls a "non-sacramental" church that meets monthly. An open-minded creative approach to fundraising can also become a means of evangelization.

Deedee pastors a Christian congregation where the church budget was perennially undersubscribed with money a topic too personal and private to talk about in public. She offered to create a series of five workshops for leaders in the congregation on the subject of "Faith, Money & Giving." Initially, her proposal was stonewalled by her board as they felt they were "too busy to take on something new." Quietly she persisted. Finally, the stewardship committee agreed to three workshops. Deedee then sent personal invitations to key leaders and members in her congregation. The response to the workshops was overwhelmingly positive. One participant gushed: "I never knew that talk about money could be so informative and nonthreatening." Then came the ultimate surprise. For the first time in memory, the fall fundraising campaign was oversubscribed by "many thousands of dollars."

Charlie is a pastor in a growing multi-generational church where his assignment includes fundraising. Charlie had no fundraising experience so he enrolled in the Executive Certificate in Religious Fundraising course offered by the Lake Institute and the Lilly Family School of Philanthropy at Indiana University. He then took a full year to design a multi-faceted program that would speak to the diverse interests of his congregation. He:

- formed a communications team, hired a digital marketing minister and raised $30,000 to fund the new position.
- helped the congregation launch a new website with an online giving link.
- created the "Real Life Café" as part of the newly renovated church narthex to highlight the mission programs and service opportunities of the church.
- developed a series of stewardship videos to be utilized in worship and on the church website.
- began the "Legacy Fund" to encourage planned giving by members of the parish.
- designed a new giving data system to more effectively and efficiently track the giving practices of each member in the congregation.

What was the result? The following year the congregation experienced a 50 percent increase in the number of people responding to the annual giving appeal.

Father Tony, the pastor of a Catholic Hispanic parish on the West Coast, took a more pastoral and theological approach. Once Father Tony caught the vision of money as a spiritual tool to be used in the service of God, everything changed. Change centered in the pulpit as Father Tony began to read the lectionary texts through an economic lens: Be we rich or poor what does it mean for us to be faithful with what God has given us? Next, he designed a series of educational programs for his parish staff, his parish council and his financial team. His goal was to increase the weekly offertory 10 percent. By the end of the year Father Tony discovered that the weekly offering had grown by nearly 30 percent.

The majority of clergy who enrolled in the Lake Institute certification program did so to prepare themselves to lead a fundraising program. At the end of the seminar almost half of those present realized that their congregations were not ready to engage in a new fundraising initiative.

First they had to step back and address some basic organizational issues. Organizational readiness turns on the willingness of a congregation to take the time and care to get key leaders and potential giving-partners onboard and on the same page!

# TABLE TALK

## For Personal Reflection

- What is your personal response to the seven questions found on page 40?

## For Group Reflection & Conversation

- What are some of the cultural traditions and fundraising practices in your congregation to which you need to be sensitive and may need to address if your fundraising is to be successful?
- Are there generational differences you need to address or programmatic silos and social networks that require special attention for your fundraising efforts to succeed?
- After reading this chapter, would you describe your board as ready to lead and worthy to receive the goodwill and gifts your congregation deserves?

## Action Steps

- Summarize your conversation relative to the above questions.
- List, then prioritize, the specific issues, challenges or concerns you discussed.
- Design a process by which you will try to address and resolve these issues before you engage in your annual fundraising or stewardship program.

---

1 Rebekah Basinger, "The Trustees' Role in Advancement: Beyond the Bottom Line."

2 Karla Williams, *Leading the Fundraising Charge.*

3 James D. McLennan,"The Board of Directors: Stewards or Guardians?"

4 The Chronicle of Philanthropy, 2013.

5 Carl Dudley & Nancy Ammerman, *Congregations in Transition*, 2002.

6 "The Generosity Project 2016," The Evangelical Council for Financial Accountability. Achieve, "The Millennial Impact Report Retrospective: Five Years of Trends," 2016. Amy Thayer, "Six New Insights on Millennials," 2016. Achieve, "Millennial Impact Report," 2013. Huffington Post, 7/8/16. "The Philanthropic Enterprise," 9/16/16. "Figuring Out the Millennial Christian Giver," Christianity Today, 6/12/17.

7 David Odom, Faith and Leadership,"Management Strategy," 9/20/16.

# (5)

# WHAT HAS GOD TO DO WITH MONEY & GIVING?

*"Money must serve, not rule!"[1]*
*Pope Francis*

Do you remember the questions you asked as a child or the questions you were asked by your children? Questions like: "But why should I share?" "Why can't I keep what I have for myself?" "Where does money come from?" These are more than children's questions; they are deep questions that taunt us for life. Ignore them and life degenerates into a narcissistic funk, tempting us to focus on getting as much as we can and keeping it for ourselves. Grapple and live with such questions and generosity becomes the roadmap to the well-lived life.

Persons of faith ask this question: "How do I give money to God and say thank you?" Many see giving to the church as the only way to give to God. Others take a broader view and see any charitable gift that addresses a human need as giving to God.[2] As historian James Hudnut-Buemler has observed, "Religious people pay to be in relation with God through the institutions they support."[3]

How ironic is the silence in many congregations when it comes to talking about God, money and giving as a Christian practice. For twelve years I began nearly every seminar I led with these two questions:

1. How many of you grew up in homes where you talked about money?
2. How many of you knew your family's income and charitable-giving practices?

In most seminars about 70 percent grew up in family's where money and charitable giving were taboo subjects. That discomfort has spilled over into the church. In a survey of church members, 60 percent said they could not recall hearing one sermon on God and money or stewardship in the last year.[4] Yet in the Bible, from Genesis to Revelation, talk about money and the faithful use of possessions is a dominant theme.[5]

> "I have, in ways that have surprised me, come to the conclusion that the Bible is indeed about money and possessions.... It is astonishing that the church has willingly engaged in a misreading of the biblical text in order to avoid the centrality of money in its testimony."
> Walter Brueggemann

Why then this silence when it comes to money? Like Father Daniel (Chapter 4), leaders often see money as having no spiritual value and consequently ignore the subject altogether. While fiscal woes are the order of the day in many congregations, the crisis is more spiritual than financial. It reflects the failure of clergy as spiritual leaders to take seriously the teachings of the Bible and speak to the angst their largely middle-class parishioners feel when it comes to money.

Writing with surgical-like deftness, sociologist Robert Wuthnow notes:

> "Churches...are often failing to address the heart issues that underlie all giving and all financial programs....They have preached tithing but have forgotten to say anything about the remaining 90 percent of their parishioners' financial burdens....To say that the problems are heart issues is to suggest that religious teaching is the central issue needing to be understood, not simply church budgets and organizational charts."[6]

The results of this silence are uninformed disciples and tight-fisted givers.

Theological integrity has to do with how we talk about God and money and fundraise in the church. Where does theological integrity begin? For clergy, it begins in the pulpit; for partnering laity, it begins at the kitchen table.

The ancient Greeks associated philanthropy/charitable giving with what they called *paideia*; schooling, education and practical training. They sensed that before people give, they must be taught. They focused on the creation of a culture honoring those beliefs that were generous, good and true. It's this notion of *paideia* that builds the bridge between the pulpit and the giving table.

I have observed that congregations with a spiritual view of money focus on the creation of a culture that nurtures a deep and holistic understanding of faith, money and giving. For example, take the question, "How much is enough?" Amidst credit card debt, monthly mortgage payments, the rising cost of a college education and angst as to retirement funds, what does it mean to handle money with care? There are no single or easy answers to these questions. Nonetheless, savvy religious leaders invite their congregations to grapple with such questions from a faith perspective with the Bible as a benchmark for wisdom and insight. At the same time, they are careful not to muddle teaching about money issues with fundraising initiatives. Joyful and generous givers are people who have grown givers' hearts before the offering plate is passed. As Martin Luther reputedly put it, conversion is a threefold path involving first the mind, then the heart and finally the purse.

What does the Bible have to say about God, money and giving? The Bible talks about money in multiple voices. Through a travelogue of historical happenings, personal stories, anecdotes, wise sayings and varied life

> **"To talk about money with biblical integrity is to take the big-picture view of what the Bible says about faith, money and giving."**

experiences, the Bible draws pictures as to what it means to live faithfully and give generously. But beware! No single text can be pocketed and twisted into a one-size-fits-all truth. The big picture must inform all our money conversations.

To talk about money with theological integrity is to take a big-picture view of what the Bible says. Lutheran theologian Mark Allan Powell says that most of what the Bible says about money and material possessions can be summed up in four words which he calls **ARMS**.[7]

**A** = *How we acquire it*

**R** = *How we regard it*

**M** = *How we manage it*

**S** = *How we spend it*

Biblical scholar Walter Brueggeman uses the phrase "the economics of generosity" to describe the big-picture view.[8] As for Jesus, while he didn't fundraise, he did talk a lot about our attitudes toward money, the fragility of money, the cunning of wealth, our care for the poor and the challenge of living generously.

Evangelical New Testament scholar David Downs reads the scriptural money story through the lens of what he calls "atoning almsgiving." This perspective uncovers a largely forgotten insight that once motivated Christian giving: There is something meritorious about charitable giving! Almsgiving (the practice of caring for the poor and addressing human need) has both a personal and powerful theological purpose. It reflects the way in which divine and human love interact  for the healing of God's creation. Almsgiving was  frequently viewed as a way of "atoning for" or "dealing with sin [as] both an individual and social" reality. So, the giving of many early Christians was shaped by the belief that care for the poor as a practice of mercy had "the potential to secure future reward and the cleansing of sin."[9]

What then is the message clergy need to reclaim if they are to talk about money with theological integrity? It is this: Money is spiritual! What we do with it matters to God as well as to us!

In his magisterial study of Money and Possessions (a must read for clergy) Walter Brueggemann describes the Bible from Genesis to Revelation as "relentless...in its focus and concern on things material."[10] When pastors ignore money-talk in their preaching and teaching, they are shortchanging their congregation's understanding of the gospel.

What does the giving partner, sitting in the pew, need to discover relative to God, money and giving? Just this: God made us to be generous givers! All that we have is a gift from God to be held in trust and used for the redemption and flourishing of God's creation.

How might clergy help donors make this discovery? There are four big-picture takeaways (theological insights) I have found helpful to people of faith as they ponder their charitable-giving decisions.

**Money and possessions are gifts from God.**

Money is not intrinsically evil! But, beware; neither is what we have, be it much or little, ours to use in a cavalier manner. We did not earn all we have, neither can most of us candidly claim that we deserve all that we have. Blunt Saint Paul put it this way: "What do you have that was not given to you?" (I Corinthians 4:7) Answer, "Nothing!" God is the great giver!

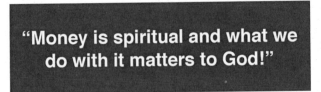

"Money is spiritual and what we do with it matters to God!"

In the second century in a homily titled "Can a Rich Man Be Saved?" Clement of Alexandria described "possessions, gold, silver and houses [as] gifts of God."[11] As Clement saw it, money was morally neutral; neither to be demonized nor deified. Likewise, wealthy people were neither to be despised nor venerated. Clement described money as an "instrument" to be put to "good use by those who know how to play the instrument skillfully." Pivotal to faith's understanding of money is what we do with it, how we handle it as a gift from God.

At the same time, there is something mysterious and bewildering about money. Never can we take for granted what we have. One day we may have it, the next day we don't. And some have more than others. In one of our seminars, a second-career pastor who had been a stock broker, grabbed our attention when he confessed: "I've made millions of dollars and I've lost millions of dollars. I have found money in itself to be meaningless, if not downright capricious."

As if to underscore that observation, the Bible tells the story of Job, a man who had everything then lost everything for no good reason. In the end, God gave Job twice as much as he had before as if to remind Job that life's fragility is "trumped by God's unutterable generosity."[12] If everything is a gift from a generous God, there is but one proper human response: Accept it as gift, hold it in trust and say "thank you!"

**Money is a fragile gift, to be handled with care.**

Not all money is the same. How we earn it and spend it shapes the social and moral character of it. The Bible is particularly sensitive to the perils of money. On the one hand, as the 16th century reformer John Calvin notes, money and possessions are "God's gifts...created for our good and not our ruin." On the other hand, he describes money and the way we use our possessions as a "slippery slope."[13] Misused, we either tumble toward miserly frugality or toward greedy self-indulgence. Ponder the story of King Solomon. God made young Solomon rich, then wealth became Solomon's obsession and the aging king's undoing. (1 Kings 3:13; 11:1ff)

In a way, money is like the lottery—alluring, intoxicating, but ultimately deceptive. Money can easily delude us into thinking that if we have enough of it we can protect ourselves from the traumas of life. Money can also corrupt and crush the moral compass. So, the Bible tells stories about people who allowed their money to own them, characterizing such people as fools!

Two stories come to mind. The first is the tale about a man named Nabal, a name that literally means "Fool." (1 Samuel 25) Nabal was a wealthy landowner who lived only for himself with a steely-cold heart when it came to feeding the hungry, caring for the poor and treating his employees fairly. One day he refused to give food to a young warrior-upstart named David who was fleeing from King Saul. Rebuffed, David was ready to take matters into his own hands when Nabal's wife Abigail intervened. She gave David the food he needed then counseled him to do nothing to even the score with Nabal. Why? In Abigail's words, Nabal was no more than an old fool living up to his name. What happens to old fools? Given enough rope, old fools hang themselves. Then the shoe drops in the storyline. Nabal suffers a heart attack and the story-teller concludes with this punchline: "then God finished him off and he died."

> "When our religious beliefs and values shape our giving, something serendipitous happens; God shows up!"

The second story is the story Jesus told of a greedy farmer. The farmer had been blessed with a bumper crop and was about to cash in his holdings and spend it all on himself when God stopped him in the dead of night, saying: "You fool! Tonight you are going to die. And your barn full of stuff — who will get it?" (Luke 12)

Death, as life's one great certainty, punctuates the transience of money. We can't take it with us! What matters to God is what we do with what we have, how we choose to use it. The sage of Proverbs puts it well: "Better to be poor and walk in integrity than to be crooked and rich." (Proverbs 28:6) Or, as my mother taught me as a child: "Hold lightly what you have because it is not yours, it's a loan from God."

**Money and possessions are to be used in neighborly ways for the flourishing of humanity.**

The great commandment has a twofold thrust: "Love God with all your heart, understanding and strength...Love your neighbor as you love yourself!" (Mark 12:30) Biblical scholar Ben Witherington reminds us that this commandment has economic implications as it is a call to love our neighbors with "exuberance and abundance."[14] The great commandment is also a heads-up summons to congregations: What difference are you making in the neighborhood where God has placed you? To live the great commandment as Jesus intimated on a visit to his hometown of Nazareth is to model an "alternative economics" whereby the borders of our neighborhoods are stretched to embrace the world God created and called "good."

Who is the good neighbor? Good neighbors are people whose giving priorities are in place: to care for the poor, the homeless, the needy, the alien, the hungry. Good neighbors are deliciously portrayed in the Bible as: "Gracious, compassionate and good...they donate and lend generously, they lavishly give to the poor...their generosity goes on and on, and on." (Psalm 112) *The Didache*, an early second-century instruction manual for Christians, put it this way: "Do not be someone who holds out the hands for receiving but who clenches the fist for giving."[15]

> "The giving table is a table of lavish grace, hearty abundance and contagious joy."

Jacqueline Fuller, director of Google's charitable arm that donates $100 million a year in grants and $1 billion in products annually, was asked what her faith had to do with her leading a charitable organization. She replied, "I remember reading the Bible when I first became a Christian. I came away thinking... God loves the poor, and we have a responsibility to ensure that we're never the oppressor, and that we're taking care of strangers and widows and orphans and the fatherless. That made me think that this is something I should do as a Christian and started me on the journey."[16]

In giving generously, we unshackle the slavish grip money has on life. Hope is born! Humanity flourishes! God smiles! Or, as the sage of Proverbs puts it: "Those who are generous are blessed, for they share their bread with the poor." (Proverbs 22:9)

**In giving, we become part of something bigger than ourselves.**

In our giving we participate in God's gracious love for creation and become the face of Christ to our neighbors. When our religious beliefs and values shape what we do with money something both intriguing and bewildering happens; God shows up!

Many of my Jewish friends use the Yiddish phrase "*tikkun olam*"—to mend or repair the world—to capture part of the mystery of giving. The phrase reflects the conviction that while God created a good world, we live in a world where things rust, break and go awry, leaving the world in constant need of repair. As a rabbi explained to me, "God created us to be givers, for it is in our giving that we partner with God in the healing of a frayed and fractured world."

A vibrant young clergywoman shared with me the story of her call to ministry. She was pursuing a career in music until her senior year in college when she began to feel a nudge to consider Christian ministry. Here was the rub: To enroll in seminary and begin her training for ministry she first had to be approved by her denomination. She did not have the money to pay her way through all the denominational tests and hoops required of a ministerial candidate. One week she shared her dilemma with a few friends, including her music teacher. The next week at the end of her music lesson her teacher gave her an envelope containing a check. The next Sunday at church an elderly man gave her another check. The checks totaled the exact amount of money she needed to begin the seminary process. "And that," Jessica said, "is when God showed up!"

The parable Jesus told of the sheep and the goats captures another part of this mystery of giving. In our giving, God shows up and we find ourselves incognito in places we've never been. Catholic theologian Gary Anderson calls Matthew 25 "the most important text for the early church" because it shaped the early Christians' understanding of charitable giving.[17] The parable suggests that it is in our giving and caring for the hungry, homeless and hurting that God shows up and we meet Christ.

It was this notion that there was something (dare I say) sacramental or Eucharistic about giving that transformed the understanding of charity in the later Roman Empire. The focus in traditional philanthropy was on the erection of public buildings, parks and statues to honor a donor. Christian charity focused on almsgiving as loving care for the poor.  Historian Peter Brown writes:

> "By bringing God Himself into human society in the form of a human being,  Jesus of Nazareth, the Christian doctrine of the Incarnation added dramatic power to the notion [that in giving generously] we find ourselves standing in the very presence of God."[18]

In giving, we become part of something bigger than ourselves! We become part of God's redemptive presence in the neighborhoods and world in which we live.

Where does a theology of giving and an economy of generosity end? It ends where it begins—at the giver's table.

First Timothy is a letter addressed to church leaders with a focus on money and giving. What does it mean for persons of faith to be responsible with what has been given to them? Good stewards share their resources generously to care for the needy and in so doing "grasp the life that is truly life." (I Timothy 6:19) Saint Paul writes: "If you want to be a leader...don't be money-hungry...handle your household affairs well.  If you don't know how to manage your own household well, how can you take care of God's church?" (I Timothy 3:3f)

Home economics—how we handle our finances—is truth telling because it reveals the ultimate beliefs that shape our giving.[19] When our Christian beliefs inform our giving, something life-changing and earth-rattling happens. The kitchen table becomes more than a giving table. It becomes a table of lavish grace, hearty abundance and contagious joy; and something serendipitous happens. In the words of Saint Augustine: "The presence of  divine greatness walks among us when it finds among us the space of charity."[20]

# TABLE TALK

## For Personal Reflection

- In what ways do you see your charitable giving as giving to God?

## For Group Reflection & Conversation

- As you read this chapter, what new insights did you gain as to what the Bible says about God, money and giving?
- Share personal stories about the times or places in your life when God showed up through the giving and generosity of others.

## Action Steps

- Outline the steps you will take to nurture a congregation that sees money  as a gift from God to be used for the flourishing of God's world.

---

1 Pope Francis, *The Joy of the Gospel*, #58.

2 Peter Mundey, Hilary Davidson, Patricia Snell Herzog,"Making Money Sacred: How Two Church Cultures Translate Mundane Money into Distinct Sacralized Frames of Giving," Sociology of Religion, Vol. 72, No. 3, 2011, pp. 303-326.

3 James Hudnut-Beumler, *In Pursuit of the Almighty's Dollar*, p. 7.

4 Robert Wuthnow, *The Crisis in the Churches: Spiritual Malaise, Fiscal Woe*, p. 29.

5 Four excellent resources for congregations and clergy on this subject are: Walter Brueggemann, *Money and Possessions.* Luke Timothy Johnson, *Sharing Possessions.* Sondra Ely Wheeler, *Wealth as Peril and Obligation:The New Testament on Possessions.* Ben Witherington III,*Jesus and Money.*

6 Wuthnow, ibid., p. 14.

7 Mark Alan Powell,"Stewardship for the Missional Church," *Rethinking Stewardship,* Word & World, Supplement, Series 6, October 2010, pp. 77ff.

8 Brueggemann, ibid., pp. 98, 241-242.

9 David Downs, *Alms: Charity, Reward and Atonement in Early Christianity*, pp. 6-10, 183, 273ff.

10 Brueggemann, p. 11.

[11] Clement,"Who is the Rich Man That Shall Be Saved?" Also see essay by Jaroslav Pelikan in *Good and Faithful Servant*, edited by Anthony Scott.

[12] Brueggemann, p. 138.

[13] John Calvin, *Institutes of the Christian Religion*, 3/10/1-2.

[14] Ben Witherington III, *Jesus and Money*, p. 151.

[15] Downs, p. 235ff.

[16] Philanthropy Magazine, "Interview with Jacquelline Fuller," Winter, 2016.

[17] Gary Anderson, *Charity*, p. 6.

[18] Peter Brown, *Poverty and Leadership in the Later Roman Empire*, p. 92.

[19] Brueggemann, pp. 239-247. Downs, pp. 146-162.

[20] Augustine, *Sermons,* Vol.III/5, p., 169.

# (6)

## FUNDRAISING AS JOYFUL PRACTICE

*"Fundraising is the gentle art of teaching
people the joy of giving!"*[1]
*Hank Rosso*

What is it about religious fundraising that is unique and special? Just this, it is religious! It is a celebration of faith. It is a form of witness and a spiritual practice. Religious values, beliefs and language should frame the entire fundraising process. The widely respected theologian Henri Nouwen captures the distinctive essence of religious fundraising when he describes it "as a form of ministry… a way of announcing our vision and inviting other people into our mission."[2] To minister is to take seriously the hopes and hurts of those who have been entrusted to our care and keeping; and this includes our giving partners.

> **"Fundraising as ministry takes seriously the hopes as well as the hurts of the donors who have been entrusted to our care."**

As ministry, fundraising is a joyful celebration reflecting what God is about within a specific community of faith. It is an activity framed in gratitude because it blesses a congregation with the opportunity to tell its story. It is also a public invitation inviting everyone to participate in God's neighborhood party.

Now, you should be ready to party! You have clarified who you are and what you are about as a congregation. You have gathered data as a witness to the effectiveness of your mission and ministry. More importantly, you have collected stories of lives changed because of what you do. You have nurtured personal relationships with your giving partners who, in their giving, are discovering that they are part of something bigger than themselves. In short, you have done your homework. Your leaders and key players are

> **"Asking is not begging! It's an invitation to partner in what God is about in your world and neighborhood."**

onboard and ready to lead your fundraising charge. Now it's time for you to harness your imagination. What would a fundraising program that is framed in joy look like in your congregation?

Why this emphasis on fundraising as a party and celebration? Lamentably, the scolding model has too frequently characterized the annual fundraising programs in congregations. This ill-fated approach has but one goal: to get the money by creating a sense of obligation through guilt and spiritual inducements. While the result may be a pledge or donation, the gift is likely to be meager and begrudgingly given. How then does a congregation turn fundraising into a joyful practice?

**First: Be transparent and personalize the way you talk about money.**

Make giving easy. Respect the reality that people give in different ways. We live in an increasingly cashless society that jeopardizes the ritual of the Sunday offering. ATMs are available in the lobbies of many evangelical congregations to provide attendees with the sacred cash they desire come the offertory.[3]  At the same time, keep envelopes available in the pews for the older generation. As for online givers, make it simple to find the "give" or "donate" button.  Encourage monthly giving via electronic banking and credit cards. Welcome those who may wish to give stock or gifts-in-kind. However people choose to give, receipt their gifts in a timely and gracious manner. In the congregation I attend my wife and I receive a letter acknowledging our pledge within a week of making our annual pledge commitment.

Be honest and accountable as to the use made of the good gifts people give you. If people choose to designate their gifts for a specific program or purpose, honor those requests. Give them periodic updates as to the difference the gift is making. Why is fiscal transparency important? Because it builds trust among your giving partners. It assures them that as a business entity as well as a church, you are worthy to receive their good gifts and know how to make good use of them.

A man who attended one of our seminars in Georgia called me from Florida. He had moved to a retirement community and was upset with the way his new congregation conducted its annual stewardship campaign. It reflected the "scolding" approach. Come Pledge Sunday the dollar amount needed was glumly highlighted with members of the congregation urged to step up and do their "fair share." But, in the weeks that followed, nary a word was spoken relative to what happened on Pledge Sunday. The pulpit was silent as the stewardship committee considered its dour work to be done. There was no public "thank you," no celebration, no acknowledgement as to the dollars raised and pledged, nothing. My friend was aghast; the ensuing silence became for him an ethical issue. "No longer," he said, "can I in good conscience contribute generously to a congregation that has no sense of fiscal accountability and feels no need to say 'thank you.'"

In your public appeals to your congregation don't just focus on your dollar goal; personalize your appeal. Use good data to breathe life into the line-item details of your budget. How many families and individuals were served last week or last year in your food pantry? How many families were counseled in bereavement (funerals) or how many couples began their lives together with God as a partner (weddings)? How many children and young people benefited from your programs and missions? Remember how Peter (Chapter 3) used Sunday school data to breathe life into his congregation's annual stewardship appeal? A gift of $700 enabled a child to attend Sunday school for a year. Tell story's that humanize the data.

Don't limit your annual stewardship campaign to a one-Sunday event. Follow up with weekly progress reports that are positive, creative and celebratory. People want to give to organizations that are successful; they want to be part of a winning team.

Remember Baptist Pastor Joe (Chapter 3) whose congregation was wading through a seismic-change both in the way they created a budget as well as in the way they raised funds for the budget? Joe sensed that many were sitting in the bleachers nursing a skeptical wait-and-see attitude. Needed were torchbearers to light the way. So, Joe met with several large-capacity partners and invited them to make lead gifts which would be anonymously announced to the congregation to spur trust and enthusiasm. Their response was positive, and the rest is history. The congregation exceeded their goal by $250,000 as numbing apprehension gave way to joyous anticipation.

Jean is the pastor of a smaller Presbyterian congregation where giving has been flat for years. To infuse new life into the annual stewardship program she introduced a matching-gift component to her congregation's annual stewardship effort. She met with several long-term members to explore their interest in providing a $5,000 match for first-time givers. The idea of providing a dollar-for-dollar match caught their imagination and they committed to match up to $8,500 in new gifts. The net result was a 25 percent increase in the 2016 church budget.

**Second: Tailor the stories you tell to the interests of the particular audience you are addressing.**

Age is a persistent challenge as many congregations have five generations among their members.[4] Obviously the same story will not speak to all these generations. Tell stories that will speak to the passions and interests of the generation you are addressing.

Gender and marital status are also distinguishing characteristics. Take your female donors seriously and give them a leadership role in your fundraising program. Single women are more generous in their giving than men. Among couples, when women participate in making the charitable decision, giving is more generous than when the man alone decides.[5] It is a truth to be honored: Donors are motivated by appeals that respect their identity and mirror their interests.[6]

Does personal wealth shape the giving of individuals and families? Recently, a group of researchers test-marketed two charitable appeals with a large group of people where the only significant difference had to do with wealth. One ad read: "Let's Save a Life Together. Here's How." The other ad read: "You = Life Saver. Like the Sound of That?" The first ad, which appealed to a giver's sense of community and responsibility, had a higher response rate from individuals with average and below-average levels of wealth. The second ad focused on the difference an individual donor might make and had a higher response rate from individuals with above-average levels of wealth.[7] However, when it comes to wealth and giving, be careful. Don't mistake wealth or the size of a congregation with generosity in giving.

# +18%

**amount of money a congregation with 100 members receives per attendee vs. a congregation with 400 members[8]**

Know your audience and personalize the stories you tell to fit the group or individual you are addressing.

A wealthy and generous donor met with Pastor Sam to discuss his giving. The conversation went like this: "Pastor, you know how much I give and you know what I am capable of giving, but I don't want our congregation to be dependent on my money for its survival. Here's what I'd like to do. I'll continue to make my annual pledge, but once a year I'd like to sit down with you to talk about other needs or special projects beyond my pledge that we might address together."

Money can be a burden. People of wealth often struggle with what it means to be faithful and generous without their giving becoming divisive or offensive. Consequently, their giving is often anonymous. Such people can become God's catalysts and dream-shapers in a congregation.

Larry was such a dream-shaper. John is the pastor of a historic urban congregation. Every summer Larry invited John to his club for a golf game. One year Larry stopped John short in the middle of his backswing with this question: "John, as you think about the future of our congregation, what is your vision for our church?" John flushed, then sliced his shot into the woods as he did not have an answer. Recovering quickly, he replied: "I'd like to think about that." The next year as they were riding in the golf cart, Larry said: "Well, John, have you been thinking about my question?" The vision John shared was not small, it captured Larry's imagination. Their conversation continued over several months with Larry eventually pledging to match dollar-for-dollar every dollar raised as the congregation embraced John's vision. Last year that congregation completed a $30 million global chase-the-vision campaign thanks to Larry's match.

### Third: Think big! Cast a wide net!

Don't handcuff God by thinking small and asking for a minimal contribution or focusing your fundraising solely on the faithful few. Make everyone feel that they have something to give.

Remember Moses (Chapter 3)? The genius of Moses was this: He made certain that there was something for everyone to bring. "Men and women alike came and brought gold ornaments of every kind, contributions of silver or copper, spun yarn and fine linen, spices and oil, etc." (Exodus 35)

> "Sow sparingly and you reap sparingly; sow bountifully and you will reap bountifully."
> 2 Corinthians 9:6

There is more to fundraising than money. Generous giving has to do with the way people use their skills and the manner in which they share ideas, practice hospitality, offer encouragement, make connections and use their time to enable a congregation to fulfill its calling. Focus your annual fundraising program on money only and you will stifle broad participation. Enlarge your vision as to what is giving and you will grow a congregation that lives to serve others.

Generosity has a boomerang effect. The more generous we are, the happier and healthier we are likely to be. What sets generous people apart is this: They are people who have a real purpose in life. They feel they have all they need and know that clinging to what they have will not bring happiness; so they share their time, money and care with others. By contrast, ungenerous people tend to lead "concave lifestyles that drain and hollow out whatever health, vivacity and happiness they might otherwise have."[9] Based on their examination of data from a 2010 national survey of nearly 2,000 Americans, sociologists Christian Smith and Hilary Davidson write: "It is now a sociological fact, in giving ourselves away we flourish."[10]

In casting a wide net, think beyond your church membership and worship attendees. Think about former members who have moved, children who grew up in your church who now live elsewhere, outside groups who make use of your facility, neighbors whose children benefit from your programs, nonmembers who serve in one of your mission outreach programs, businesses who value your presence in the neighborhood and community. Find ways to draw them into your fundraising circle.

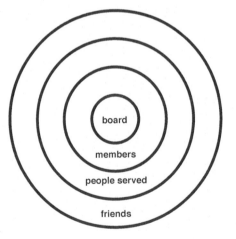

Why don't more people give? The most common answer is, "I've never been asked!" Don't be afraid to ask, but personalize the ask. Think about the person you are asking. Know why you are asking and what you are asking for. A piece of Biblical wisdom comes to mind from James, who tradition calls a brother of Jesus. James is talking about prayer but his insight is relevant to fundraising. He begins: "You don't have because you don't ask." Then comes the caveat, "You ask and don't have because you ask with bad intentions to waste on your own cravings." (James 4:2-3) Asking is not begging; it's an invitation. An invitation to partner and share in what God is about in your part of God's world.

One caution! Do your homework before you embarrass yourself or your prospective donor. When seeking a gift from an individual for a particular mission or project, is there a rule of thumb to guide? From my colleagues at the Fundraising School, which is part of the Lilly Family School of Philanthropy at Indiana University, I learned the wisdom of what is called the LAI principle.[11]

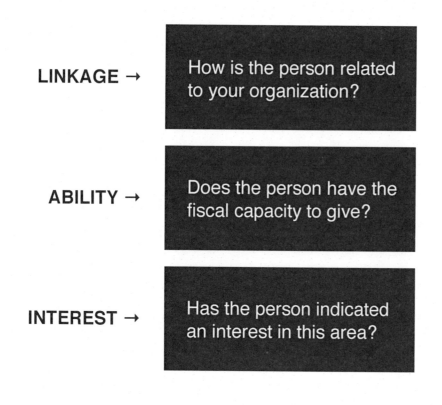

**LINKAGE →** How is the person related to your organization?

**ABILITY →** Does the person have the fiscal capacity to give?

**INTEREST →** Has the person indicated an interest in this area?

Linkage has to do with relationships. What is the relationship between the prospective donor and the special program for which you are seeking support? If there is a relationship and you are soliciting a lead or larger gift, you will then need to ascertain the fiscal ability of the donor to give the gift you seek. Finally, there is the question of personal interest. While your prospective donor may have the capacity to meet your ask, is the program for which you are seeking support of interest to your donor? Fundraising is as much an art as it is a science!

Fundraising is like a mysterious treasure chest as, on occasion, a door unexpectedly opens to God's surprises. There is no other way to put it; sometimes God inexplicably drops handkerchiefs out of the sky and a donor appears, as if out of nowhere.

Such was Don's experience. Don was the pastor of a congregation in a semi-rural community. One day the mail brought him a thousand dollar check from a stranger who lived out of state. The note accompanying the check simply read: "Thank you for what you did for me as a boy." Don did the next right thing. He promptly sent the man a "thank you" note expressing his gratitude as well as his curiosity as to the reason for the gift. A year later, Don received another check, this time a much larger gift in which the individual stated that as a boy he had attended the church, the Sunday school, the youth group, the Boy Scouts. His childhood experience had formed his faith and prepared him for life. His check was his way of expressing his gratitude. The fundraising moral: Cast a wide net because we never know what surprises God has up God's sleeve.

**Fourth: Say "thank you" and do it with joy.**

Several years ago I was leading a day-long seminar for an organization of executives serving Lutheran nonprofit organizations. We were talking about the importance of being accountable to donors as to how their gifts were used and the difference their gifts were making. Suddenly and inexplicably a question popped into my head I had never before asked a group of laity. "Tell me," I said, "you are all active in your churches; have any of you ever received a letter or note from your pastor thanking you for your annual contribution to your church?" An audible sigh wafted the room as but three of seventy people raised their hands. Then came the head-nodding response: "If pastors only knew how to say 'thank you' church giving would change."

How does a pastor and church say "thank you?" One Methodist pastor on the West Coast put up a big tent in his back yard and invited the larger giving partners in the congregation to dinner. The invitation did not state the reason for the dinner. People came expecting the pastor to make a new fundraising appeal. Instead, he caught everyone off-guard when he said that this was a Celebration Dinner, a time for him to say "thank you" to the people of his congregation. A pastor in Texas began to host small "thank you" dinner parties in her home. My own practice as a pastor was to send a personal "thank you" note in January to everyone who had made a financial gift to the church in the previous year. I also made personal telephone calls to our more generous givers throughout the year. Each quarter a statement of giving was sent to each member of the congregation accompanied by a letter in which I thanked members for their support and highlighted, via story and data, the impact their generosity was making in changed lives.

Where does the idea come from of religious leaders sending "thank you" letters to their givers? It's older than you think, and goes as far back as Saint Paul. The New Testament Letter to the Philippians is a "thank you" letter to Paul's donors. It was a letter intended to be read aloud in public worship for everyone to hear. It's a model "thank you" as Paul's message oozes joy and gratitude. It's been called Paul's "happy letter." It begins (Phil. 1: 3-4) with Paul expressing his gratitude for the ways in which the Christians in Philippi have financially supported him in his ministry. It is also a letter illuminating Paul's theology of fundraising.

> "It is in their giving that donors often find their calling."

As Paul saw it, the generous people in Philippi were not giving their money to him, they were giving their money to God. Via their giving they were linking arms with Paul as together they partnered in Christ's ministry.

The letter ends with a concluding "thank you" (Phil. 4:10-29) in which Paul turns the generosity of the Philippians into a joyous liturgical act. He describes their gifts as "a fragrant offering" that puts a smile on God's face. For Paul, arm-twisting and obligatory giving were alien to the spirit of the gospel. Paul writes: "God loves a cheerful giver." (2 Corinthians 9:7) Giving is joyful when we see our giving to be a reflection of God's cheerful generosity.

What is the key to joyful and generous giving? In my search for an answer, my African-American brothers and sisters have been my best teachers. The first time I visited a black church I was taken aback—shocked would be a better word—by the manner in which the offering was celebrated. Never, had I experienced anything comparable. Offering time was neither boring nor routine. As the offertory music began, the ushers proceeded down the aisles in rhythmic dance step. Then, as the ushers took their places at the front of the church, all across the room people began to glide to the front where the ushers were standing. It was a glorious moment of high energy as people of faith sashayed forward to give their tithes and offerings to God.

Years later, I was convening a consultation of national church leaders representing the diversity of the Christian faith. The Lake Institute was in its infancy. The purpose of the conference was to help us discover the status of faith and giving in the various Christian traditions. The first evening a glumness fogged the room as it became clear that the money issue was sobering in most traditions. Then a lonely voice spoke up: "Ya'll know what you need to do? Ya'll need to go out and get yourselves some drug addicts and tell them about Jesus." And a haunting silence wafted the room. The speaker was George, the pastor of a dynamic Missionary Baptist Church in Florida with a multimillion dollar budget and a membership that included millionaires as well as more than three hundred recovering addicts.

George then told this story. An addict came to him one day with this question: "How do I say thank you to God for my new life?" George talked about what it meant to live life faithfully and well. He also talked about the tithe as a way of expressing gratitude to God. The addict gasped: "Preacher, you mean that God don't want but a dime out of each dollar? Why the street dealer, he wants the whole dollar!" "And that," said Pastor

George, "is why come Sunday morning when it's offering time, there's a log jam at the tithe box."

A recent survey confirms George's wisdom: "Donors are ten times more likely to give to a ministry that shows the love of Jesus."[12] A primary principle underscoring Christian fundraising is this: Don't downplay Jesus!

What is congregation-based fundraising? It is the joyful celebration as to what God is about in the neighborhood your church calls home. Saint Augustine, reflecting on Psalm 42, compares life "In the house of God" to "a never-ending festival….[a place where] the angelic choir makes an eternal holiday….as our hearts hear a melodious melody that charms the ears."[13]

Now, it's time for you to reflect the joy of the gospel via your fundraising, and hear the angels sing!

# TABLE TALK

## For Personal Reflection

- What word comes to mind when you think back on the way your congregation approached fundraising in the past? Now that you have a new way of envisioning fundraising, what word or words would you hope people might use to describe your new vision of stewardship?

## For Group Reflection & Conversation

- Share with each other your responses to the questions you addressed in your personal reflection.
- List the various social groups, program interests and generations you need to pay attention to for your fundraising to be effective. What stories might you tell to speak to these special interests?

## Action Steps

- Based on your group conversation, design an annual fundraising festival for your congregation that will inspire cheerful giving and transform your annual appeal into a joyous celebration.

---

1 Hank Rosso is the founder of the Fundraising School at Indiana University, Lilly Family School of Philanthropy. See: *Achieving Excellence in Fundraising*, p. 4.

2 Henri J. M Nouwen, *The Spirituality of Fund-Raising*.

3 James Hudnut-Beumler, "Why Cash Remains Sacred in American Churches," The Conversation, June 21, 2017.

4 Haydn Shaw, *Generational IQ: Why Christianity Isn't Dying*.

5 Women's Philanthropy Institute, Indiana University, "Women Give, 2016."

6 Judd B. Kessler & Katherine L. Milkman, "Identity in Charitable Giving," The Wharton School, University of Pennsylvania, 2014.

7 Ashley Williams, Eugene Caruso, Elizabeth Dunn:"How Wealth Shapes Responses to Charitable Appeals," Journal of Experimental Psychology, December, 2016.

---

[8] National Congregations Study, 2015.

[9] Christian Smith & Hilary Davidson, *The Paradox of Generosity: Giving We Receive, Grasping We Lose.* pp. 114, 222.

[10] Christian Smith & Hilary Davidson, pp. 224ff.

[11] The Fundraising School, "Principles & Techniques of Fundraising," Lilly Family School of Philanthropy, Indiana University.

[12] "The Generosity Project," 2016, The Evangelical Council for Financial Accountability.

[13] St. Augustine, "Exposition on Psalm 42," Church Fathers.

Made in the USA
Lexington, KY
21 August 2018